HOW TO MASTER SELF-HYPNOSIS IN A WEEKEND

THE SIMPLE, SYSTEMATIC AND SUCCESSFUL
WAY TO GET EVERYTHING YOU WANT

RICK SMITH - HPD DHYP

ricksmith**hypnosis**.com

I am a certified clinical hypnotherapist. I am not a doctor or medical practitioner, and I do not offer medical advice or diagnosis. You are free to use hypnosis as you see fit, however if you have any doubts concerning it's efficacy in your case, you should seek guidance from a qualified medical practitioner.

This book offers free access to downloadable audio recordings.

CONTENTS

PREFACE

There are plenty of books about Self-Hypnosis, so what makes this one different?

Maybe you're trying self-hypnosis for the first time, or maybe you've tried before and failed. Whatever the case, you're looking for *results*, otherwise you may waste your time and come away disappointed and disillusioned. You need a system.

In this book, you'll learn;

- How to master simple self-hypnosis techniques, so that you can relax into a comfortable trance, anywhere, anytime.
- How to use your new self-hypnosis skills for relaxation and recreation.

- How to use self-hypnosis to control stress, and to centre yourself.
- How to attack bad habits, such as smoking, drinking, over-eating; in fact, anything that you feel the need to change.
- How to empower yourself for motivation, focus and commitment.

You'll also discover how to avoid the common mistakes that many people make;

- They don't practice often enough, so they fail to master the key techniques.
- They don't get the *set-up* right, so they're easily distracted.
- They hold on to their inhibitions, and never release their restrictive self-control.
- They analyse and over-think, rather than letting nature do its best work.

By eliminating these issues at the start, your chances of success are hugely enhanced.

Using this book (and the free audio recordings that come with it) you'll learn exactly the same techniques I train and use with my personal clients, for a fraction of the cost and time. I will guide you through the process, you'll go at your own speed, and if you follow the system, you'll find success. Who knows where it might lead you?

With regular use, you'll acquire a powerful secret weapon that will serve you in almost any aspect of your life. And the more you do it, the better you will become.

It's easy, it's free, and it's really fun to do!

ABOUT THE AUTHOR

Rick Smith graduated as a Certified Clinical Hypnotherapist in 2007, and holds the NCH Hypnotherapist Practitioner Diploma from the Surrey Institute of Clinical Hypnotherapy. He works with private clients around the world and also utilises applied hypnosis and neurolinguistic techniques in commerce and industry, both online and offline. In addition to his commercial consultancy, Rick writes, records, and publishes on hypnosis and related subjects.

More than thirty audio download hypnosis programs,

covering subjects like anxiety, confidence, procrastination, insomnia, and stress, can be found at www.ricksmithhypnosis.com

f **◎**

HOW TO USE THIS BOOK

Self-hypnosis can't be learned just by reading about it.
There! I said it.

I spent years researching an effective self-hypnosis method that I could teach my clients, and one that could also be trained online. I read a lot of books, and what struck me was the avalanche of theory and explanation that the reader needed to wade through before getting to the meat of how to actually *do* self-hypnosis.

By deconstructing the techniques that we clinical hypnotherapists are trained to use, I developed a more direct, no-nonsense self-hypnosis system, using audio-recordings - the *Scripts* - to enhance the training process and give my clients ongoing access to the material, in order to continually sharpen their skills.

This method has been tried by well over twenty thousand people, and I can see from the download activity that many of them use the recordings over and over. The feedback is overwhelmingly positive - this stuff really works!

If you're going to *master self-hypnosis in a weekend* - which is our objective - then spending hours digesting the history, psychology and personal opinions of the author is counter-productive. You probably want to get on with it, and try it for yourself.

So this book consists of two halves: first, how to do it, and second, how to use it.

In a moment we're going to dive straight in and start learning self-hypnosis itself. In later chapters you'll be able to read about specific ways to apply your skills, and even some of the theory behind how hypnosis works. But for now, what's important is to start learning about how to achieve *hypnotic trance*, so that you can repeat and practice the self-induction, and get better and faster at reaching the place where the changes will happen.

There's an interactive table of contents so that you can jump around inside the book, if that's the way you like to do things. Alternately - and I recommend this - you can follow the book in chapter order, which will rapidly equip you with the necessary skills and techniques, and then let you personalise and develop the self-hypnosis experience according to your own requirements.

By far the best and most efficient way to *install* self-hypnosis (in the absence of a real-life hypnotist) is to use an external sound-track; a *script* if you like. There are three scripts in this process;

1. **Basic Induction.** This first script will allow you to experience hypnosis and trance, maybe for the first time in your life. You can repeat it as often as you like, and the more you use it, the more comfortable and confident you'll become with the whole hypnosis process. You don't have to do anything except relax and enjoy the experience.

2. **Calibration.** In the second script, you'll explore your own capabilities whilst in trance. You'll discover your *modality*; how you see, hear, and feel whilst hypnotised. Once again, you may repeat this session several times, and your depth of trance and imagination skills will improve each time.

3. **Installing Self-Hypnosis.** In the third script, you're now ready to receive the essential tools which will enable you to do it for yourself, using simple triggers that you'll learn. How would it feel to have such a simple and effective way of controlling stress or anxiety, changing bad habits, overcoming nerves, or simply relaxing and exploring?

Using The Scripts and Recordings

Each of the scripts is printed long-hand in the book. If you want to, you can read and record the scripts yourself. If you want a quicker fix (maybe you prefer not to listen to your own voice) I've recorded them for you, with my voice, and you can download or stream these recordings free of charge, using one of the links in the book.

I recommend you use your smart-phone, mp3 player, or tablet computer as the quickest and most convenient method. You can carry the recorded scripts with you, so you can use them anywhere, anytime. I've included instructions about how to do this on Apple and Android devices, and I'm sure if you are a Windows, Sony, or Blackberry user, you will be able to adapt these instructions for your own device.

If you encounter any issues, please e-mail me at rick@ricksmithhypnosis.com and I'll fix it for you. A few of the book's reviewers complained that they couldn't access the scripts in the past, and punished me with one or two stars. These issues are invariably down to a user's own security settings, so if you mail me you'll get a quick solution, and I'll avoid any more negative reviews!

You can use the same scripts on an iPod or any other MP3 player in more or less the same way. If you don't use a portable device, you can play the recordings from your

PC or Mac. Somewhere in the world, somebody's probably listening to them on a cassette player or even an 8-track. Let me know if it's you!

You can download or stream the scripts by using the link at the end of this section. You'll receive an immediate e-mail with your access details.

Repetition is a key strategy with hypnosis of any kind, and you'll discover lots of opportunities to drop into trance and practice your skills. Full instructions about how to use these scripts, either streaming live or recorded for portability, are included in Chapter 2.

Everything you need to know, and everything you need to do, is laid out in sequence. All you have to do to succeed is to follow the system.

If you enjoy the book and you find it useful, please take a moment to post a Review. When *Master Self-Hypnosis in A Weekend* was first published in 2013, there were maybe twenty books on the subject. Now there are hundreds, and most of them are disappointing, so if you find this book worthwhile, please help others to discover it by reviewing it. Thanks.

Now, just relax and enjoy the ride.

Here's where to go to download the recordings. Just type it (carefully) into your internet browser, and follow the on-screen instructions.

http://tiny.cc/mshpbreg

1

THE MASTER SELF-HYPNOSIS SYSTEM

When you set out to learn anything new, the most important factor that will determine your success is the *system*. Self-hypnosis is no different. If you approach it in a haphazard way, you may have some limited success, but it will take you longer. You may get frustrated with your lack of progress, and quit before you even get to the interesting parts. So, in order to achieve your goals and objectives, you should follow a blueprint which sets out the various stages.

The method we're going to use comprises a *three-stage* system. Ideally, you'll be able to devote a weekend to this coaching course. If you allocate the right amount of time, and take the exercises in the correct order, by the time you have completed the three stages you will be quite capable of dropping into your self-induced hypnotic state at will. You will have made inroads into whatever aspect of hypnosis brought you to this book in the first place. Each stage involves a series of repetitive exercises, which are designed to consistently increase your confidence and competence, and deliver the results you seek. Successful hypnosis is all about *conditioning*, so it's important to repeat and recycle the experience.

If you follow the instructions and complete the exercises, you will achieve the following:

Stage One: You'll experience hypnosis (guided by my voice) and become confident in your ability to achieve a hypnotic trance state.

Stage Two: You'll practice *visualisation* in trance, and discover your primary *modality*. Now you'll be experiencing the power and potential of hypnosis.

Stage Three: We'll then install the skills and techniques of self-hypnosis, so that you can drop in and out of trance, virtually at will.

Stage One

In the first stage, you're going to use my 'plain vanilla' hypnosis induction script, in order to experience the actual state of hypnosis for yourself. Although you will be controlling the hypnotic process, I will be guiding you in the same way that I would if you were sitting in the chair in my office

Either play it on your computer, or your phone or tablet, through headphones. If you choose to record the written script for yourself, that's fine too. But why go through all the hassle of making the recording when the audio script is easy to access and completely free?

Click on the link, or copy it into your browser. You'll be asked for your name and e-mail address, and then you'll receive an e-mail with your private access details to download or stream the recordings, as often as you like, for as long as you like.

You will try this initial exercise a minimum of three times. Each time that you repeat it, the process will become easier and more natural. The objective is to build your confidence in the hypnotic process itself, and to convince you that hypnosis works for you.

Remember we're not trying to do anything complicated at this stage. We're just demonstrating that you can be hypnotised, and that it's a pleasant and relaxing state.

Each repetition of this exercise will take no more than fifteen minutes, so with breaks in between for a cup of tea, you can complete Stage One in around two hours.

If you're committing to Master Self-Hypnosis in a Weekend, you might do this stage on Saturday morning, and then you can break for lunch. You're embarking on a fascinating adventure which will equip you with a really powerful new skill by the end, so it is really worthwhile to set the right amount of time aside, and focus only on completing this first exercise, before you do anything else in your 'real-life'. Don't worry if you're not feeling it for the first couple of tries. Just persevere (like relaxing is *such* hard work!) and it will come.

Stage Two

This time, there's a script which is designed to guide you in *visualisation*, a really useful skill to develop if you are going to make the most of your hypnotic adventure. If you can teach yourself to visualise well, you can use this power for many different applications.

This script (called 'Beach') will also enable you to discover your *primary modality*, that is to say are you mainly (though rarely exclusively) visual, auditory, or kinaesthetic (feeling). Knowing this will help you to design your *trance work* according to your own personal strengths.

Stage Three

By the time you reach Stage Three, you should be getting pretty good at entering hypnosis on your own. The *conditioning* will have started to take effect, and each time you decide to go into trance it will be quicker, and you will find that you can go deeper than the last time.

*You've organised your mind to **expect** and **anticipate** the hypnotic state.*

In this stage, we're going to use the skills you've practiced, and a new script. This time we're going to work together to *install* the techniques for self-hypnosis, so they'll be hard-wired in your brain for you to access whenever you need them..

If you've read other books on the science, you might reasonably have asked yourself the question *"How am I going to remember what I have to do, when I'm supposed to be in trance?"*

I agree, this is a daunting prospect and it's the reason why people often fail to achieve their goals. I've written several books about learning script-type information, and I can promise you that you will not be able to absorb and implement the long scripts that some hypnosis trainers would have you use in self-hypnosis. You don't need to work that hard to get great results.

The structure of hypnotic language is based on a system which takes professional hypnotists several years to perfect, so to expect to you to be able to remember these rules and then work on yourself in trance is, in my opinion, beyond the reasonable capabilities of most people. So again, I will guide you through the process, and together we will install the basic techniques and then practice them until you can easily do it yourself.

In this stage, we'll repeatedly practice dropping in

and out of trance, deepening the state, and freely exploring your sensations and impressions whilst you are in hypnosis. Here you'll be taught how to use *triggers* and *anchors* to relax quickly into a comfortable trance, whenever the opportunity or need arises.

Once you've completed these three stages, you may have everything you need. However, if you'd like to delve deeper into the origins and basis of hypnosis, and explore the many different ways in which you can use self hypnosis to improve your life, you'll enjoy Part Two.

Recreation, Contemplation, Meditation

Now that you're able to enter hypnosis at will, you may already have achieved your personal objectives. By dropping into trance, you place yourself in the ideal situation to explore your own mind on almost any subject of your choosing. All you have to do is to decide what you want to investigate, and once you have completed your self-induction, you are free to spend as much time as you wish exploring the deep recesses of your mind.

Many people, once in this state, find that answers to long-standing questions reveal themselves. Others report that they're able to find order in chaos, and to re-organise their views or feelings on matters that have been confused or unclear.

This book, and the script recordings, will give you

instructions and techniques to focus on dealing with these challenges using your own self-induction, so that you can do your 'routine' any time you feel the need.

Hypnotherapy

If you're attracted to hypnosis because of more significant issues in your life, it's likely that you'll need to employ more elaborate techniques, probably based on recorded scripts. You will have conditioned yourself to drop easily into hypnosis; however you will need professional guidance to achieve more ambitious therapeutic goals once you are in trance.

There are numerous resources available online to help you approach issues like Smoking, Weight Loss, Phobias, Addictions and so on. In the Appendix you will find recommendations for commercially available download services which can provide scripts for virtually any issue you care to name.

Your First Time in Hypnosis?

For the purpose of this exercise, we'll assume that you've never been hypnotised before. Even if you have, you should still follow the directions. You may have been given instructions and advice in the past: it may have been good advice, or it may not. Here is a brief insight into what we will be trying to achieve at this first attempt.

Fundamentally, hypnosis is all about achieving the deepest possible state of physical and mental relaxation. The idea is that you 'switch off' your responses and reactions to external stimulation, and your conscious 'critical faculty', that aspect of your brain which evaluates and analyses things that you see, hear and feel.

When you achieve this condition (the *trance*) you are able to directly access your powerful sub-conscious mind, which is where your learned habits and behaviours are stored and managed. Then you can make changes to the way you do things, and *anchor* the changes, so that they become new embedded habits and behaviours.

But before you can start to do this kind of work on yourself, you need to become good at the actual hypnosis part. So this first exercise will teach you how to approach self-hypnosis in the right way, and give you an initial experience of how it feels. If you follow the instructions correctly, you will achieve a level of hypnosis which may be deep or shallow.

You won't really be in a position to judge your *depth of trance* the first few times you do this. In fact you may not even feel that you are hypnotised at all, but as you repeat the exercise you will definitely begin to notice an improved experience each time. Hypnosis is progressive. Each time you decide to go into trance, you will be stripping away your natural resistance and becoming more comfortable and inquisitive about where it will take you 'this time'.

So in the first exercise we are going to use a simple induction script, similar to that which a professional hypnotist might use in a consultation. This script is designed to enable you to achieve a reasonable level of trance very quickly, and if you use it a few times, especially over a short period such as a morning or an afternoon, it will work better and deeper each time you do it.

Remember, this exercise is solely designed to allow you to experience the hypnotic trance state for yourself, nothing more. You'll be going in, hanging around for a couple of minutes, and then coming out again. Next you'll be repeating it as soon as you're ready, as many times as you like, until you are completely comfortable with the way it works for you. By the time you've done the exercise four or five times, you'll be well ahead of the script, and you'll going deeper and deeper each time.

So, if you're ready, go get Exercise One. Here's a reminder of the link if you haven't done it yet...

http://tiny.cc/mshpbreg

2

PREPARATION AND SET-UP

In this chapter, we're going to look at two important practical aspects of Self-hypnosis;

- How to access and use the recorded scripts, using your computer, smartphone or tablet,
- Preparing and setting up your self-hypnosis environment.

How to Use the Scripts.

The first script we are going to use is called 'Exercise One; Basic Induction and Emerge' and (to repeat) it can be found in your download package.

It's an MP3 file, which means it will play on just about any device, and it's around 15MB, so it's really quite small.

It lasts around 15 minutes. You can use it in a number of ways;

Record It for Yourself – The Hard Way

In the next chapter, the script is printed long-hand. You can read and record it yourself, using your smartphone's Voice Memo or Voice Recorder function (or any other recording device), and then play it back as many times as you need. It's that simple, though if you want to be really clever with this, save the recording with a name (I suggest you use the title above) and then access it through iTunes or your music application. If you use Android instead of Apple, the instructions are more or less the same.

If you are using your smartphone as the recording device, the easiest and most effective way to record your own voice is to use the microphone attached to your hands-free headphones. This avoids you having to hold the phone and gives you easier access to the controls. You will be able to pause and re-start the recording as needed.

However, listening to your own voice is not always ideal, and you probably don't have experience in reciting hypnosis scripts, which rely for their effectiveness on certain voice techniques. So, although this is a perfectly practical way to work with the scripts in this book, I seriously recommend you use my pre-recorded versions as explained below. You will get a better result and it will be much quicker to get started.

Using My Scripts – The Easy Way

Stream to your Smartphone or iPod

If you prefer to use my pre-recorded script, you can start it by clicking on the link in your Welcome E-Mail.

If you click, copy, or type the link into your phone's web browser, you can play the file directly from the web. This means you can access it from anywhere that you have data access, though I would recommend you don't use contract data with your phone carrier unless you have a large or unlimited data bundle. Wi-fi, particularly at home, is usually free, so that's the best and most reliable way to access the script.

Whenever you use your phone for playing scripts, which you'll be doing a lot throughout this course, please use headphones for privacy. This also helps to block out external noises which can be a distraction during your Self-hypnosis sessions.

Download to your Computer

You can use your computer's web browser, by copying or typing the link, and the audio file will open (it may start to play). I recommend you pause the audio, then right-click on it, selecting *'Save Audio As'*. This should open a file saving dialogue box, and you can download and save the MP3 file in your music library. Once you've done that, you can open your music player (such as iTunes) and find the track in the alphabetic list of all your stored music tracks. The artist name is Rick Smith.

Alternately, if you download it to your 'Downloads' or 'Desktop', you can then open iTunes or your preferred music player, and import the file from there.

You can play it from there, or alternately you might decide to create a new Playlist (call it "Self Hypnosis") and drag the track into it. Then you will easily be able to find it, and when you sync to your phone or tablet next time, make sure you add the playlist and you'll be able to find it easily on your device, which is where you really need it to be.

To repeat - if you hit a snag, email me on rick@rick-smithhypnosis.com and I can provide you with an alternative link, usually within a couple of hours, depending on your time zone.

Set-Up and Preparation

In order to give yourself the best opportunity for success with self-hypnosis, we need to pay attention to your immediate environment. The more ideal we can make the set-up, the more relaxed you will become and the fewer distractions are likely to occur. Most of these instructions are simple common sense, but you'd be surprised at how many people ignore the obvious!

Privacy

In the early stages, whilst you're learning the basics, you need to shut yourself away somewhere private, and make sure you won't be disturbed. Self-hypnosis is a solitary pastime; the clue is in the title: *self-hypnosis*, and there's nothing to be gained by having someone else listening in or involving themselves in the process.

If you live alone it's simple. If you have family, particularly a parent, sibling, or partner, it's up to you if you decide to tell them what you are planning to do. However, it's always better to come clean, because when you finally shut yourself away to practice you really need to have eliminated any concerns that you are doing something covert or sneaky, or that someone might think of you as foolish or flippant if they accidentally discover what you are doing. Hypnosis always works better if you are free of short-term worries. You don't want to be trying to induce a trance whilst keeping one ear open for approaching footsteps!

Whatever the case, they need to understand that whilst you are practicing self-hypnosis, they should not disturb you unless the house is burning down! As for kids – well, I think you know the answer to that! But seriously, if you are going to eliminate distraction, which is necessary for this process to work, you must *control your environment.*

Tranquillity

Silence in your hypnosis environment is ideal, though it may be impossible to achieve total peace and quiet, especially if you live in a city. Nevertheless you should strive to establish the quietest possible space for your self-hypnosis.

Close the doors and windows and switch your phone to 'Flight Mode' so that it won't ring or vibrate. Anything which disrupts your concentration whilst you're doing the exercise will necessarily take you back to the beginning. Once you are well-practiced at this, you'll be able to deal with external sounds as part of the trance, but at the beginning, until you've mastered the process, you need to eliminate as much external disturbance as possible.

Pets can be a particular problem, especially dogs. I

once visited a client in her home, and I was quite concerned to find that she had an open plan house and four pet dogs, including two huge German Shepherd guard dogs who barked like crazy when she tried to shut them outside. I decided that the lesser of two evils was to have the dogs in the lounge with us whilst we did the session.

They spent the whole hour licking her, climbing on and off chairs, and generally making a nuisance of themselves. I'd travelled a long way to see her and she was paying a lot for the therapy, so I was forced to improvise by incorporating the dogs into the hypnotic induction, so that she was able to ignore them. It took a little longer than usual to get her into a workable trance, but I stuck at it and the session was, in the end, completely successful. However, I am a trained professional and I know how to do these bizarre things from time to time. I doubt you'll be able to manage anything like this when you are doing hypnosis alone, so don't try.

If there are sounds in the room, such as a ticking clock (preferably you should move it or stop it temporarily) an air-conditioning unit, or anything else, you need to take some time in your preparation to get used to the ambient sounds, because you may have never really listened to them before. The idea is that you merge all sounds into the general environment so that they do not become intrusive. Once you get your trance going, you will either not notice them at all, or alternately they may simply become part of the comforting aspects of your environment.

Remember, you should be using headphones to listen to the scripts in this first phase. If you are using ear-buds, external sounds will break through quite easily. However, if you can use a pair of over-ear or even noise-cancelling headphones, external sounds should not be a problem. I regularly used headphones for my clients and a headset microphone for myself in my London practice, which is just 2000ft underneath the flight path for Heathrow airport!

Your Personal Comforts

As you've understood, achieving the *hypnotic trance state* will always go better if you eliminate distractions, which includes physical distractions. Wear clothing that doesn't pinch or constrict (you may want to remove your shoes, belt, and watch). Please make sure you visit the bathroom before you start, because a call of nature half-way though your session is difficult to ignore, and it will probably require you to start the induction all over again. Make sure the room temperature is comfortable; not too cool and not too warm.

Where to Sit

If you visit a professional hypnosis practitioner, you will rarely see a couch or flat-bed in his or her office, and there is a good reason for this. As you can imagine, taking people into a state of deep relaxation can run the risk of them falling asleep, especially if they arrive tired for the session. If you're lying down, the risk is increased, because this is most people's natural sleeping position. If a subject nods off during hypnosis, the session is essentially wasted, because the aural senses shut down as soon as you are asleep and nothing goes in, apart from the noise of a fire alarm or a wake-up!

Falling asleep during hypnosis is not uncommon, and it is completely harmless. Once asleep, the hypnosis is over, and anything that happens whilst you're asleep won't be effective.

Within the scope of the hypnosis exercises you'll do in this course, you can be sure that you will eventually wake up 'out of trance', so no harm done. But you could waste some time and effort, which is why you should try to avoid lying horizontally if possible. Of course, if you have no alternative comfortable location, the hypnosis itself will work fine on a couch or bed, but you need to be aware of the heightened risk of snoozing through the best bit!

The ideal situation is a comfortable chair: a recliner if you have access to one. A Lazy Boy is not ideal, unless you can lock out the leg-rest, because the very best seating position for hypnosis is to have your legs uncrossed and your feet flat on the floor. You should make sure your head and neck are supported if possible. Where to put your hands is really related to how you would normally sit to relax. I've found that most clients like it if I give them cushion to put on their lap and then they can rest their hands on it.

A competent professional hypnotist can work on clients in almost any position, and if you've ever seen a good stage hypnotist, you'll have seen subjects put into trance whilst standing up. This is genuine, but it takes training to master. For your purposes, you should try to get as close to the picture as you can manage. As long as you're comfortable, and you don't need to tense any muscles to maintain your position, this will work just fine.

Stimulants

Stimulants can be an issue, so you should avoid them. Coffee in particular can inhibit relaxation, so it is best to avoid drinking it at all on the days you're going to work on your self-hypnosis skills. Later, once you've mastered dropping in and out of trance at will, it won't make much difference. But in the early stages, you're trying to eliminate every possible obstacle to you being able to enjoy the relaxation state that leads to hypnotic trance.

If you're a smoker, especially if you're learning hypnosis in order to help you quit, I recommend that you thoroughly cleanse your breath and hands before you start. In hypnosis, senses can sometimes sharpen unexpectedly, and the smell of tobacco could become intrusive once all other distractions are suppressed or eliminated, which could trigger a craving.

Of course – and this probably goes without saying – alcohol and drugs don't go well with hypnosis. It's virtually impossible to hypnotise a drunk, and although I did once manage to put a stoner into a deep trance, after many attempts, the work we tried to do once he was hypnotised was completely ineffective because I was battling mental forces I have not been trained for! Other drugs are mainly stimulants, and it's pointless to try.

Light and Dark

It doesn't really matter how light or dark your environment is, though given the choice I would always prefer to use hypnosis in a darker room. You may have to open and close your eyes a number of times during the process, and if the room is bright this can tend to kick you out of trance more quickly because of the contrast when you open your eyes to the light. How dark is really a matter of personal preference. During the day you should close your shades or blinds so that there is still natural light in the room, but no bright light source. If you're practicing in the evening, a side-lamp is better than a bright ceiling lamp. Try to make sure it's out of your line of sight.

That's just about it for your environment. Most of these tips are obvious, but they all combine to create the most conducive situation for you to succeed at self-hypnosis, so try to consider each one in terms of its practicality for you.

So, you've got your script ready, and you're seated and relaxed in a comfortable, private environment.

You're all set, so let's get on with the first exercise.

3

STAGE ONE, SIMPLE INDUCTION AND EMERGE

What You'll Be Doing

In this first exercise, we're going to use a standard hypnosis induction to start to get you used to how hypnosis works.

If you've visited a professional hypnotherapist in the past, it's possible that the 'induction' part of your session may have been quite a prolonged affair. Many therapists use a technique called 'progressive relaxation' to take you gradually into a light trance, and then slowly deepen the state over anything up to an hour. This works fine for most people, but it takes a long time.

Rapid Induction

A famous American hypnotherapist, Dave Elman, having observed the apparent need to repeat this long-winded conditioning exercise, developed a very successful alternative which accelerates the induction process. I have been using this 'Elman Induction' with clients for several years, and found that it works every time. This induction compresses the repetitive conditioning into a series of brief 'mini-inductions' which start to induce a trance, then 'wake up' the subject, before repeating the process again and again. The technique ensures that each time the subject opens his or her eyes, then drops back towards the trance state, they go deeper.

The result is a nicely hypnotised subject in a matter of a few short minutes. This is the technique we will be using in our Stage One Exercise.

Deepening Your Trance

Once this part of the induction is completed, we will use what is known as the *Escalator* technique to deepen the trance. Again, this is a short procedure, which involves visualising a descent towards what we can call your *basement of relaxation* where both mind and body are fully relaxed.

In the first exercise, this basement is where we will

rest for a few minutes, to allow you to explore the sensations and clarity which hypnosis offers. At the beginning of this pause you will be offered suggestions of things you can do, however what is most important is that you take time to enjoy the tranquillity of the hypnotic state. You will not be expected to make any earth-shattering discoveries at first, however each time you repeat this exercise you will find that you'll become more confident and inquisitive.

Whilst you're in your basement of relaxation, you may find that you can begin to visualise scenes, places, or events. Alternately you may experience feelings, which can often become quite intense. How you'll experience hypnosis will depend on you as an individual, whether you're principally visual, auditory or kinaesthetic by nature, or maybe a combination of any or all of these.

After an appropriate period of quiet time, the script will begin again and you will be gently emerged from your trance state, until you're wide awake, back in the room, and feeling great.

During Your Trance

Despite what you may have heard, hypnosis is completely safe, and you will never lose your ability to wake yourself up if you feel uncomfortable with what's going on. The likelihood is that you will wonder about this, sometime during your experience, but you'll feel so good that you won't feel the need to try to wake yourself up. I invite you to test this for yourself once you've gone through the induction stage.

There are three accepted stages of hypnotic trance which most professional hypnotherapists use. For the purpose of this explanation, we'll call them *light, medium, and deep*. You'll find a more detailed explanation of these trance states in the second part of the book. In professional practice, the *deep* state is often used for treating really serious psychological conditions, as well as medical and dental anaesthesia.

It's unlikely that you will ever reach a state of deep (*comatose*) hypnotic trance using self-hypnosis. Even if you do, the techniques contained in these scripts will work in exactly the same way, to emerge you back to your full waking state when it's time.

In this first exercise, we'll be targeting the *light* state. In this state, most people remain fully aware of where they are and what is going on around them, but they choose to 'switch off' that consciousness and 'go inside' to explore their own internal thoughts, images, and feelings.

You may achieve this light state on your very first attempt. You may even recognise it when it happens, or you may perhaps feel that nothing has changed, and you're just relaxing in a chair with your eyes closed. It doesn't matter, because you're going to repeat the same exercise several times, and each time you go into hypnosis you will go deeper than the last time, and you'll find new sensations and experiences which will encourage you to go further.

Remember, it's a *conditioning* process, and the more often you do it, the better you'll become.

When you emerge from your first hypnotic experience, we're going to conduct a little de-brief, so that you can reflect on how you got on.

So, make yourself comfortable, put on your headphones, and when you're ready, start the recording.

Here is the script, in case you've opted to record it for yourself. If you're using the pre-recorded script, you can skip this section completely:

∼

Exercise One Transcript

When you're ready to enter hypnosis, take a long deep breath and hold it for a few seconds. As you exhale this breath, allow your eyes to close and let go of the surface tension in your body. Just let your body relax as much as possible right now.

Now, place your awareness on your eye muscles and relax the muscles around your eyes to the point they just won't work. When you're sure they're so relaxed that as long as you hold on to this relaxation they just won't work, hold on

to that relaxation and test them to make sure <u>THEY WON'T</u>
<u>WORK</u>.

Now, this relaxation you have in your eyes is the same
quality of relaxation that I want you to have throughout your
whole body. So, just let this quality of relaxation flow through
your whole body from the top of your head to the tips of your
toes.

Now, we can deepen this relaxation much more. In a
moment, I'm going to have you open and close your eyes.
When you close your eyes, that's your signal to let this feeling
of relaxation become 10 times deeper. All you have to do is
want it to happen and you can make it happen very easily.
OK, now, open your eyes... now close your eyes and feel that
relaxation flowing through your entire body, taking you much
deeper. Use your wonderful imagination and imagine your
whole body is covered and wrapped in a warm blanket of
relaxation.

Now, we can deepen this relaxation much more. In a
moment, I'm going to have you open and close your eyes one
more time. Again, when you close your eyes, double the relaxation you now have. Make it become twice as deep. OK, now
once more, open your eyes ... close your eyes and double your
relaxation... Good. Let every muscle in your body become so
relaxed that as long as you hold on to this quality of relaxation, every muscle of your body will not work.

In a moment, I'm going to have you open and close your
eyes one more time. Again, when you close your eyes, double

the relaxation you now have. Make it become twice as deep. OK, now once more open your eyes... close your eyes and double your relaxation... Good. Let every muscle in your body become so relaxed that as long as you hold on to this quality of relaxation every muscle of your body will not work.

Now, that's complete physical relaxation. I want you to know that there are two ways a person can relax. You can physically relax and you can relax mentally. You already proved that you can relax physically, now let me show you how to relax mentally.

In a moment, I'll ask you to begin slowly counting backwards, in your mind, from 100. Now, here's the secret to mental relaxation; with each number you say, you'll double your mental relaxation. With each number you say, let your mind become twice as relaxed. Now, if you do this, by the time you reach the number 97, or maybe even sooner, your mind will have become so relaxed, you will actually have relaxed all the rest of the numbers (that would have come after 97) right out of your mind. There just won't be any more numbers. Those numbers will leave, if you will them away. Now, start with the idea that you will make that happen and you can easily dispel them from your mind.

Now, in your mind say the first number, 100 and double your mental relaxation. Now the next number..... Good.... Now double that mental relaxation. Let those numbers already start to fade. Next number.....Double your mental relaxation. Start to make those numbers leave. They'll go if you will them away. Now, they'll be gone. Dispel them. Banish them. Make it happen, you can do it, Push them out. Make it happen! THEY ARE ALL GONE

That's fine. The mind is relaxed and the body's relaxed. Just let yourself relax much more with every single breath. And I do want your body to relax just a little bit more so let me help you do that. This time I will count from 5 down to 1. With every number I say, let your mind and body relax together like a team so that by the time I reach the count of one, mentally and physically you easily let yourself relax much more. All right?

5-deeper--that's good—4 - 3 --that's fine-2 – deeper down and --------------- 1.

That's great, doing fine. I'd like you now to see if you would allow yourself, to let yourself, to go to your very base-ment of your ability to relax. And you know there is no real basement of a person's ability because we've never found a basement, only on every particular instant in time your base-ment can be many, many times deeper. And I'll help you to get there.

I want you to imagine that there are three more levels to take you to your basement of your relaxation.--levels -A, B, and C. To get to-level A,- you--simply- double the relaxation that you have now. To get to level B, you must double the relaxation you have in level A. And finally to get to your base-ment, you must at least double what you have in level B. To help you with this, I want you to use that powerful imagina-

tion of yours. And I want you to imagine that you're standing at the top of your own private escalator, like they have at the shopping centre only this is your own private escalator.

I am going to count to 3 - and at the count of 3, you'll step onto your escalator that will be taking you from where you are now down to level A, double the relaxation that you have now. When you get there, you'll let yourself know by simply raising one finger gently. Here we go-1-2-3. Step on to the escalator and go down, deeper down, doubling that relaxation which feels so good. When you reach the next level, step off your escalator and relax. Good, wonderful.

Now in a moment we're going to go from level A to level B. To get to level B, you simply have to double the relaxation that you're allowing in level A. Just let it grow twice as deep. All right. Imagine yourself at the top of your next escalator. Here we go, 1-2-3 and step on... Let it take you all the way down where you will have doubled your relaxation. Now, if you're following these instructions, you may find it difficult to move your finger, but that doesn't matter at all. But try anyway. Just take all the time you need to get to level B--- and when you arrive at the bottom of that escalator, step off and relax. Good.

Now there's one more level that I'd like you to go to: Level C -- the very basement of your ability to relax. Once more, find yourself at the top of that escalator. At the count of three, step on and it will take you all the way down to level C -- the very basement of your ability to relax today. Here we go: -1-2-3. -deeper-deeper-letting go-

deeper-deeper-deeper-to the very basement of your relaxation-drifting down-much more relaxed. OK. That's fine. Way down. Now just let yourself stay there for a moment and notice at this level every breath you exhale just easily helps you relax even more. Every breath takes you deeper and deeper relaxed.

Now as you relax, drifting deeper with every word I speak, the first thing I would like you to know is how much I appreciate and admire you for the decision you have made to try hypnosis for yourself and to explore the wonderful benefits that it can add to your life.

Now you have those physical signs that allow you to know that you have moved from one conscious state to another in a calm and confident way. In this calm and confident state you can offer yourself generous portions of self confidence... large helpings of self-esteem, breathing out self-doubt as you relax even deeper and continue to enjoy the journey towards your goal.

Now you're going to take a short period of silence, relaxed in this beautiful hypnotic state, and experience whatever comes to you. See what you see, hear what you hear, feel what you feel, and simply let the waves of physical and mental relaxation wash over you.

(Silence for two minutes)

You've done great. PAUSE. I'm going to count from ONE up to THREE. At the count of three your eyes are going to open, become fully alert, totally refreshed. Any cobwebs that you might have had, any sleepiness of mind is going to dissolve and disappear, and you're going to feel bright eyed and full of energy. You'll be fully alert and wonderful and marvellous in every way.

ONE, slowly easily and gently feel yourself coming back up to your full awareness, At the count of TWO you're still relaxed and calm but notice that your eyes under your eyelids feel as if they're clearing, kind of like they're being bathed in a sparkling cool mountain stream, you feel GREAT. On the next count those eyes are going to open, totally alert, fully refreshed, just feeling excited, wonderful, in every way, and every time you go into hypnosis you can let yourself go deeper than the time before because you know that just feels good. All right, get ready, and on the count of THREE open those eyes and notice how good you feel.

~

Welcome back!

How was that for you? Why don't you have a stretch now, I'm sure you feel like one. You completed the exercise really well.

Now, just take moment to reflect on what happened. You might remember everything, or you might remember nothing at all. It may have seemed like a really short time, or alternately you might feel like you've been gone for ages. I can tell you that the whole exercise took less than fifteen minutes.

When you're completely ready, you're going to start the recording again and repeat the experience, but this time you will easily go much deeper into hypnosis, and each time that you do this you will be able to go deeper still.

Right now, I suggest you get up and walk around for a few minutes, maybe have a cup of tea or a glass of water. Remember, no coffee and preferably no smoking! Then when you're ready to try it again, come back and make yourself comfortable.

De-Briefing Yourself

After the first time you try the exercise, there may be things that you noticed which you can change in order to make it easier next time. Just run through the check-list below, and make any adjustments before the next repetition.

- Temperature: was I too warm or too cold?
- Comfort: how was my seating position, the position of my hands, and so on?
- Volume: was the recording too loud, too soft?
- Brightness: do I need to lighten or darken the room?

- External sounds: was I distracted? Do I need to stop anything, close any windows, and so on?

These are small things, but any one of them can detract from the overall experience, so it's really worth taking a little time to get everything right, so that there are no obstacles to you achieving that wonderful depth of relaxation which hypnosis offers.

You can go on repeating this exercise as many times as you like! You will be the best judge how well it's working for you, and you'll notice the progressive conditioning as you try it again, and again. Although my voice is guiding you, the actual hypnosis is coming from you. You are allowing it to happen, and it is happening. That's the essence of self-hypnosis.

You should not think about moving on until you're entirely comfortable with this first exercise. Many people report that the second time they do it, it's much more effective than the first, and this is the conditioning effect we discussed earlier. Just keep repeating the recording as many times as you like. There's no such thing as too much practice!

Next, in Stage Two, we're going to use the skills that you've developed in Stage One to train you to use the hypnotic state to do new things.

4

STAGE TWO: CALIBRATION - A DAY AT THE BEACH

Welcome back. I hope you had a nice lunch!

Exercise Two

Now we will use another recorded script which starts off with the same rapid induction we used in Stage One.

Once you're in trance, you will be given a *trigger word*, which is 'BEACH' and your task is to experience everything associated with being at a beach. The idea is to *calibrate* you so that you will be able to tell if you are predominately *visual*, *auditory* or *kinaesthetic*. How you experience the beach will determine what we call your *modality,* and this will then be the primary way that you will approach specific exercises whilst in hypnosis.

You will be using your powerful imagination, which is allowing you to roam freely in hypnosis. If you are primarily visual, you may be able to generate a clear image of the beach scene and to be able to describe it, either during the trance or afterwards.

Maybe you will be primarily auditory, in which case you may hear the sounds of the waves, or children playing in the sand.

Alternately - if you are primarily kinaesthetic - you might feel the breeze on your face, or smell the salty air. It's entirely possible that you may experience more than one of these modalities, which is great, however it's important is to find out which is your dominant sense, so that you can then utilise it in future self-hypnosis.

It's called "Exercise Two : Self-Calibration" which you can download or stream just the same as the first one. Much of the script will be familiar to you, which should help you to drop into trance very easily. However, some of the parts are shortened because you simply don't need all the techniques now that you've become proficient. Again, if you insist on recording your own scripts, it's written out long-hand below.

Once you have the script, make yourself comfortable and quickly run through the checklist below;

- Switch your phone to Flight Mode if you've

downloaded the script. If you are going to stream it (over wi-fi) select the setting which leaves the wi-fi on but turns calls and text messages off.

- Make sure you won't be disturbed for around half an hour.
- Visit the bathroom if you need to.
- Take a few moments to acclimatise yourself to any sounds that you may hear during the exercise, and explain to yourself that these will not disturb you.

When you're completely ready, start the recording and enjoy the trance!

Here's the transcript if you are recording for yourself, otherwise you can skip this section:

Self-Calibration Transcript

When you are ready to enter trance once more, take a long deep breath and hold it for a few seconds. Now exhale this breath and allow your eyes to close and let go of the surface tension in your body. Just let your body relax as much as possible as you've done so many times before.

Now, place your awareness on your eye muscles and relax the muscles around your eyes to the point they just won't work. When you're sure they're so relaxed that as long as you hold on to this relaxation they just won't work, hold on to that relaxation and test them to make sure THEY JUST WON'T WORK.

Now, this relaxation you have in your eyes is the same quality of relaxation that I want you to have throughout your whole body. So, just let this quality of relaxation flow through your whole body from the top of your head to the tips of your toes.

Now, you know that can deepen this relaxation much more. In a moment, you're going to open and close your eyes. When you close your eyes, that's your signal to let this feeling of relaxation become 10 times deeper. You want it to happen and you have proved that you can make it happen very easily. OK, now, open your eyes... and close your eyes and feel that relaxation flowing through your entire body, taking you much deeper. Use your wonderful imagination and imagine your whole body is covered and wrapped in a warm blanket of relaxation.

Now, you can deepen this relaxation much more. In a moment, you're going to open and close your eyes one more time. Again, when you close your eyes, double the relaxation you now have. Make it become twice as deep. OK, now once more, open your eyes ... and close your eyes and double your relaxation. That feels SO good. Let every muscle in your body become so relaxed that as long as you hold on to this quality of relaxation, every muscle of your body will not work.

In a moment, you're going to open and close your eyes one more time. Again, when you close your eyes, double the relaxation you have now. Make it become twice as deep, as you did so many times before. OK, now once more open your eyes... and close your eyes and double your relaxation... excellent. Let every muscle in your body become so relaxed that as long as you hold on to this quality of relaxation every muscle in your body just will not work.

Now that you're totally physically relaxed. You are going to easily relax mentally. You already proved that you can relax physically, now you know exactly how to relax mentally. In a moment, you'll to begin slowly counting backwards, in your mind, from 100. And with each number you say, you will double your mental relaxation. With each number that you say, let your mind become twice as relaxed. Start to count, and by the time you reach the number 97, or maybe even sooner, your mind will have become so relaxed, you will actually have relaxed all the rest of the numbers right out of your mind. There just won't be any more numbers. Those numbers will leave, if you make them go away. You have proved that you can make that happen and you can easily dispel them from your mind. Now, start counting backwards from 100 and make those numbers disappear. Each number that you say will double your mental relaxation. Start to make those numbers leave. They'll go if you will them away. Now, they'll be gone. Dispel them. Banish them. Make it happen, you can do it,

Push them out. Make it happen! Good, THEY ARE ALL GONE

Well done. Your mind is relaxed and your body's relaxed. Just let yourself relax much more with every single breath. And I do want your body to relax just a little bit more so let me help you do that. This time I will count from 5 down to 1. With every number I say, let your mind and body relax together like a team so that by the time I reach the count of one, mentally and physically you easily let yourself relax much more. All right?

5-deeper--that's good—4 - 3 --that's fine-2 – deeper down and ---------------- 1.

That's great, doing fine. Now that you are so relaxed, you're going to go even deeper, and you already know how to do this. Imagine the escalators which will carry you down towards the basement of your ability to relax even deeper.

You know that there are three more levels to take you to your basement of your relaxation.--levels -A, B, and C. AS you go deeper to each level double the relaxation that you have now. Use that powerful imagination of yours so that you're standing at the top of your private escalator and when I count to 3, Step on to your escalator and it will be taking you from where you are now down to level A, double the relaxation that you have now. When you get there, you'll signal by simply raising one finger gently. Here we go-1-2-3 and down you go, deeper into relaxation. Good, wonderful. (Pause)

Now in a moment we're going to go from level A to level B

just like before. To get to level B, you simply have to double the relaxation that you're allowing in level A. Just let it grow twice as deep. All right. Imagine yourself at the top of your next escalator. Here we go, 1-2-3. And step on. Let it take you all the way down where you will have doubled your relaxation. Just take all the time you need to get to level B--- [WAIT]--Good.

Now there's one more level that you know you can go to: level C--the very basement of your ability to relax. Once more, find yourself at the top of that escalator. At the count of three, , it'll take you all the way down to level C -- the very basement of your ability to relax. Here we go-1-2-3. Step on... -deeper-deeper-letting go-deeper-deeper-deeper-to the very basement of your relaxation-drifting down-much more relaxed. OK. That's fine. Way down. Now just let yourself stay there for a moment and notice at this level every breath you exhale just easily helps you relax even more. Every breath takes you deeper and deeper relaxed.

And now you know how amazing and easy it is to get to this deep place of relaxation, and you are welcome to remain in this beautiful place as long as you want and to come here again any time that you like, because you KNOW how to relax your body and mind completely and let go so you relax so completely.

Now you have those physical signs that allow you to know that you have moved from one conscious state to another in a calm and confident way. In this calm and confident state you can offer yourself generous portions of self confidence... large helpings of self-esteem, breathing out self-doubt as you relax even deeper and continue to enjoy the journey towards your goal.

Take a few moments to appreciate the peace and tranquillity in this deep place that you have brought yourself to. (Short Pause)

Now, imagine you are at the Beach and it's a lovely day. (Pause) See what you see, hear what you hear, feel what you feel. Take a moment to experience how it is, there at the beach. Allow your powerful, wonderful imagination to transport you there and be at the beach, however that is for you.

If you can see where you are, say "I can see it", or if you can hear the sounds around you say "I can hear it" and if you can feel the warmth, the breeze, and the texture of the sand, say "I can feel it". Go on, just say out loud what is happening to you, and your imagination of this wonderful beach will grow stronger. Allow yourself to feel how good it is to be at the beach, how relaxed and comfortable you are and just rest there for a few moments, taking it all in.

(Pause)

And now you know new things, and that knowledge empowers you. You know about this beach, and how wonderfully relaxing it is to be here, and you know that you can return here any time you choose because you have proven the power of your wonderful imagination and your amazing ability to bring yourself to this wonderful state of deep relaxation any time that you choose, so easily. And I want you now to remember what happened to you at the beach today, what you saw and what you heard and what you felt, so that you can remind yourself later about this amazing beach and your clever ability to come here again. Just relax quietly for a few moments and take it all in.

(Silence for two minutes)

Now it's time for you to leave the beach for now, so let your imagination gently fade. You've done great. PAUSE. In a moment I'm going to count from ONE up to THREE. At the count of three your eyes are going to open, become fully alert, totally refreshed. Any cobwebs that you might have had, any sleepiness of mind is going to dissolve and disappear, and you're going to feel bright eyed and full of energy. You'll be fully alert and wonderful and marvellous in every way. ONE, slowly easily and gently feel yourself coming back up to your full awareness, At the count of TWO you're still relaxed and calm but notice that your eyes under your eyelids feel as if they're clearing, kind of like they're being bathed in a sparkling cool mountain stream, you feel GREAT. On the next count those eyes are going to open, totally alert, fully refreshed, just feeling excited, wonderful, in every way, and every time you go into hypnosis you can let yourself go deeper than the time before because you know that just feels good. All right, get ready, and on the count of THREE open those eyes and notice how good you feel.

∽

Welcome Back. I hope you had a nice time at the beach! Take a stretch and grab the book, so that we can review what just happened.

De-Brief

If you followed the preparation instructions and stuck to the recorded script, you should be quite amazed by now at your own ability to enter trance and what you can do whilst you're there. The Beach scene usually evokes powerful imagery or sensations in everyone who tries this exercise, and I'm sure you experienced that too. If, for some reason, it wasn't as vivid or literal as you had hoped, don't worry, just repeat the script again, even two or three times, and the effect will increase as you get more proficient at exercising your powerful imagination.

You'll remember from the introduction that this was called a 'Calibration Exercise' and the idea was to try to discover your modality, that is to say are you predominately visual, auditory or kinaesthetic. Your experience at the beach should have given you a good idea of this.

Did you see the colours? Were they bright or dull? Did you see movement, or was it like a post-card? If any of these statements are true for you, make a mental note of the answers so that you can build your future visualisations around your strengths.

Maybe you didn't see much, but you heard the sounds. Could you hear the waves, the seagulls, the people talking and kids playing? Maybe you heard a more elaborate sound-track, like a beach bar or a restaurant with music. Again, try to recall what you were hearing and make a mental note of how vivid it was, how complex and/or realistic the experience.

Or maybe you mainly felt *things*, like breeze, smell, or texture? Maybe what you experienced was an 'impression' of the beach, enough to convince you that you were there, even though you couldn't see or hear very much? That's called kinaesthetic.

You should now be able to assess and decide your dominant *modality*. If you can't do it yet, I suggest you run the recording again, now that you know what to expect, and spend some more time at the beach!

You will have accomplished this part of the mission when you are able to say to yourself: "I am predominately visual/auditory/kinaesthetic."

Remember, you don't have to have only ONE modality, but you should try to identify your dominant one, because that is the way that you will design your exercises when you start doing more interesting things in your trances.

By now you should be dropping easily into trance, and you should be totally confident in your own ability. You can completely let go and enjoy the experience, and you should also have convinced yourself that each time you do it, you go deeper.

Take a break. In the next chapter, we are going to install the self-hypnosis *post-hypnotic suggestion*, so that you will add instant self-hypnosis to your rapidly increasing skill-set.

5

INSTALLING SELF HYPNOSIS

As I said at the beginning of this book, it's challenging to teach yourself self-hypnosis just by reading some written instructions. It's a lot quicker and more effective if you have some help. It's very common for a hypnotherapist to 'install' self-hypnosis when you visit him or her for any reason. Once you've had your hour in the chair, the changes will stick a lot more effectively if you have some way of reinforcing them when you're on your own.

We're going to follow that proven method, but you can expect it to be even more effective because of the time you've already spent getting familiar with hypnosis.

Let's just run a quick check over what we've done, and what you've achieved so far:

In stage one, you were *induced* into progressively deepening states of trance. If you followed the system correctly, you will have experienced a peaceful, pleasant state of hypnosis as you repeated the exercise over and over. The key objective of this exercise was to prove that you're fully capable of entering into and emerging from hypnotic trance, and that the more often you tried, the better and easier it became for you.

In the second exercise, you again went into trance using a recorded script, and you imagined being at the beach. This was to demonstrate to you the power of your imagination: your natural ability to create realistic situations and experiences whilst you are in the hypnotic state, and also the practical calibration to find out if you are predominately visual, auditory or kinaesthetic. Knowing this about yourself will help you a lot, if and when you start to use your self-hypnosis skills for specific purposes later on.

You're now ready to receive the great wisdom that brought you here in the first place!

Exercise Three

Next, we'll use yet another script, which is designed to *install* the process for you to start to self-hypnotise. Again, we'll use a short induction to get you into trance, which you should be finding very easy by now.

Once you're in the hypnotic state you'll be given a series of instructions about how to prepare yourself, the next time you want to enter hypnosis. You'll then be invited to experience these simple steps according to the *modality* we established in the previous exercise. You'll also give yourself a *post-hypnotic suggestion,* which is a memorable 'cue word' to use each time you want to go quickly into trance.

Choosing Your Cue Word

This post-hypnotic suggestion is a powerful device, so you need to choose a word, or short phrase, which is not in regular daily use. The last thing you want is to find yourself drifting into trance in the middle of a normal conversation, or whilst listening to the radio, because someone inadvertently used your cue-word! Unlikely, I grant you, but if you've ever watched a good stage hypnotist, you'll have seen this stuff in action.

Using this cue word as a trigger to enter hypnosis will become a habit, and the more you use it, the easier and more effective it will become. Personally, I use *"And.... Descend!"* as my own cue word. I've been in and out of trance so many times that all I have to do is say it, and breathe out, and my body knows exactly what to do.

My favourite use, which crops up almost daily, is simply to calm myself in stressful situations. Living in a city like London, there are plenty of those!

You can use the same one, if you like (unless you're a

submariner or a pilot) or you can choose one of your own: it really doesn't matter. Just make sure it's unique to you.

Once we've installed the self-hypnosis technique into you, and you've implanted your cue word or trigger, you'll then emerge from hypnosis feeling wide-awake as before, and knowing that you now have everything you need to go deeper into hypnosis, any time and every time you choose.

Afterwards you can put the recordings to one side, and practice self-hypnosis for real. Remember, the more often you use it, the better you'll become, so you can simply repeat going in and out of trance as often as you like.

You'll be given some pointers on things that you might like to try whilst you're in self-induced trance, so that you can find out how easy or hard it is to give yourself suggestions. Some people are able to carry quite complex procedures into the hypnotic state. But most use it only for very simple 'one-liners', to address things like focus and concentration, motivation, calmness, and so on.

And if none of these things appeal to you, you may be one of those people who simply wants to use self-hypnosis for recreation or relaxation.

How It Will Work

In this exercise, we're going to place you in trance – much more quickly this time – and install the simple skills to enable you to self-hypnotise without the use of recorded scripts. This is really easy, and it won't take long. Once you emerge from this trance, you will have everything you need to start practicing self-hypnosis without my help.

The next script recording is called 'Exercise Three: Installing Self-Hypnosis'

Remember Your Cue-Word?

In a moment, you're going to make yourself comfortable, run through the usual check-list, and prepare to be hypnotised again. However, before you start to relax this time, you need to select your cue-word, which you will be using in the future to start the self-hypnosis process.

You'll remember that I use *"And... Descend!"* as my cue word, and you can use it too if you like. Alternately, please choose something for yourself: make it simple, easily memorable, and personal to you. Choose it now, because you'll be taking it into the trance with you, ready to use just before you emerge.

Have you chosen it? Good!

So, once we've completed the induction this time,

when you've reached the *basement of your relaxation*, you'll be given a series of instructions which you will use in the future when you want to achieve self-hypnosis. This set of instructions will be the way that you induce trance in yourself in a similar environment to the one you're currently using with the scripts.

In effect, you will have the skills to replace the scripts (although of course you can use them any time you like, if you're feeling lazy). The way that these instructions will be presented will be a kind of 'trance within a trance' where you will be using your imagination to go through the whole process of self-hypnosis. By doing it this way, you should be able to experience the sensations of self-induction with total clarity, which will successfully embed the process in your subconscious memory, enabling you to repeat it later with complete confidence and competence.

You will then emerge yourself from self-hypnosis, *but only as far as the script-induced trance that you were in before you learned the self-hypnosis instructions.*

You'll remain deeply hypnotised whilst we will give you the *post-hypnotic suggestion*, so that you can use your chosen cue-word to drop into trance any time you like. Once that's done, the recorded script will emerge you to your full waking state once more.

The duration of this exercise is around twenty minutes.

So, make yourself comfortable, check all the environmental factors, and prepare yourself to be hypnotised one more time. Here's the transcript if you are recording for yourself, otherwise you can skip this section:

Start the Script:

Installing Self-Hypnosis Transcript

Now you've done this many times before, so just take in that deep breath, hold it for a moment, and as you exhale that breath just allow your eyes to gently close and let go of the surface tension in your body. You know how to let your body completely relax.

Now, concentrate on your eye muscles and relax them until they just won't work. Test your eyes if you want to, but of course you already know that they just won't work. Good. Relax. Let that quality of relaxation that you have in your eyes flow through your whole body from the top of your head to the tips of your toes.

Now you know exactly how to double and deepen that relaxation, so on three you will open your eyes and close them again; Ready: One, Two Three, open your eyes and close them, and as you close them this time you will drift much deeper and feel that relaxation flowing through your entire body, taking you much deeper. You know how good it feels to go into this beautiful relaxed state and you really want to go deeper, so go there (Pause). Now your whole body is completely and totally relaxed and detached from your mind, so just park your body there. You don't need it until later, and you can come back to it any time you want.

Now you know how good it feels to relax your mind as well, so as you listen to the rhythm of your breathing, slow and steady, you can start to count down from one hundred, ninety nine, ninety eight and so on whilst each number doubles your mental relaxation and the numbers just evaporate until they aren't there anymore.

So now you know that you have achieved complete mental relaxation. Well done, you are really very good at this now, and you can do it for yourself in the same way, any time that you want to go into this wonderful hypnotic state, and it will be deeper and more successful each and every time that you do it.

Now you know that each time you have gone into hypnosis it is deeper than the time before and this will continue as you take control of the hypnosis for yourself, using your powerful subconscious mind.

In a moment you are going to allow your own powerful imagination to take over this process so that you can go deeper than ever before. Here is how you will do this every time you want to enter hypnosis.

Now I want you to use your imagination in a new way. You are in control of yourself.

Imagine yourself seated comfortably in your chair or lying on your couch or bed, and you are ready to enter self-hypnosis, *and you are really looking forward to it because you know how good it feels.*

Imagine that you are ready, and that you are closing your eyes, paying attention to any sounds or sensations that are happening around you, but they won't distract you because you will be completely relaxed in mind and body. Now imagine that you are paying attention to the rhythm of your breathing, in and out, and in and out, and as you breathe in and out you feel yourself becoming more relaxed with every breath, your body becoming limp and relaxed as you release all the tension from your muscles, with every breath you inhale and exhale. You have made a decision to enter hypnosis and you are really looking forward to it because you know how good it feels.

In a moment you are going to start to count down from ten to one. You may count in your mind or you may speak the numbers aloud, it's OK, and with every number that you count down you will go deeper inside yourself, doubling your relaxation with every number. And once you have no more numbers you can still go deeper just doubling your relaxation with every breath.

(Pause)

Now you are very deep inside yourself and your mind is open to new ideas and suggestions, and when you come here again you will be able to give yourself new suggestions and explore these new ideas because you have the power and imagination to do anything you want to do when you're in this place. And you can take some time now to explore and imagine how it might be for you when you come to this wonderful relaxed place any time you like, now or in the future.

(Pause)

Now that you have this power installed you can congratulate yourself because you have done something very special, and you may think that everyone should be able to do this because it feels so good, and now that you know how easy and satisfying it can be to reach this deep level of relaxation and understanding, you can tell yourself that for now it is time to start to bring yourself back. In a moment you will start to count up from one to ten and when you reach ten you will be back where you started just a few moments ago, still in a deep state of mental relaxation and with the new experience of knowing exactly how to bring yourself back to this wonderful relaxed place any time you want to.

So, when you're ready, start counting from one to ten, slowly or quickly, silently or out loud, and when you reach ten you will remain in trance with your eyes closed and your body detached, and ready to receive some final important instructions.

(Pause)

That's good: you're doing very well so far. Perfectly in fact. Now, you have been trained how to hypnotise yourself any time you like, and you have passed the course with flying colours. And each time you want to do this, you will be able to begin to relax simply by using a Cue Word, the word you brought with you. If you can remember the word you chose, say it now to yourself.

(Pause)

And each time you say that word to yourself you will be able to go deeply into self-hypnosis and each time you go into hypnosis you will be able to go deeper than the time before, and this is your personal pleasure that you can use any time you like by just using your word, say it again to yourself.

(Pause)

Now, once again you've done great. PAUSE. Shortly I'm going to count from ONE up to THREE. At the count of three your eyes are going to open, become fully alert, totally refreshed. Any cobwebs that you might have had, any sleepiness of mind is going to dissolve and disappear, and you're going to feel bright eyed and full of energy. You'll be fully alert and wonderful and marvellous in every way. ONE, slowly easily and gently feel yourself coming back up to your full awareness, At the count of TWO you're still relaxed and calm but notice that your eyes under your eyelids feel as if they're clearing, kind of like they're being bathed in a sparkling cool mountain stream, you feel GREAT. On the next count those eyes are going to open, totally alert, fully refreshed, just feeling excited, wonderful, in every way, and every time you go into hypnosis you can let yourself go deeper than the time before because you know that just feels good. All right, get ready, and on the count of THREE open those eyes and notice how good you feel.

And... Stretch!

De-Brief

So, what we did there was have you go through the procedure of hypnotising yourself, whilst you were already in hypnosis. If this sounds a little strange to you, don't worry. This method works very well, because it teaches you the simple steps that you'll be using yourself.

However, by doing it whilst you're already in trance, the instructions are accepted by your subconscious mind without question, so that when you come to execute the procedure for yourself from the normal waking state, you will automatically know that it's going to work, and you will have total confidence in your ability to achieve an excellent state of trance all by yourself.

If you're comfortable with what you've just learned, then you can move on to the next stage, in which you will practice self-hypnosis without a script. If you would like a little more coaching before you take the next step, you can replay the previous script as often as you like. The advantage of repeating it, even just one time, is that you will know what to expect, so if you experienced any obstacles or confusion the first time around, now is the time to eliminate those completely.

6

PRACTICING SELF-HYPNOSIS

Next you're going to use what you just learned, and practice hypnotising yourself for the first time. Here's a reminder of the steps you'll take;

Seat yourself comfortably and run through your check-list to make sure you won't be disturbed or distracted. Listen for any external sounds and accept them, telling yourself that these sounds will not disturb you during your trance.

Think about what you would like to do once you are in trance. Maybe you will be taking some silent time to contemplate nothing in particular, just to see where it leads. Or maybe you have a specific topic you would like to take a look at whilst you're under, in which case try to establish how you will start that process, using either a well-formed image or an internal description of a feeling or sentiment. We'll talk more about this later, but for now, just give yourself a simple starting point that you will be able to use once you're ready. Pictures are good.

Tell yourself that you are ready to enter hypnosis and that when you are finished you will be ready to come out again and feel great. You can speak this aloud or silently say it to yourself.

When you're ready, take a deep breath, hold it for a few moments, and as you exhale, say your cue word and close your eyes.

Start to count down from ten, synchronising the counting with your breathing, so that with every breath you exhale, you double your physical and mental relaxation and go deeper inside.

When you've counted down to one, you will instinctively know if you have fully relaxed your body and mind. If you feel you need to go deeper, use the escalator visualisation that we did in the previous exercises. Go down as many levels as you want, always telling yourself that as you descend, you will be going ever deeper into that wonderful trance state. You will remain completely aware of your own thoughts; however you can detach your mind from your body and leave your physical self on any of the levels until you are ready to come back.

When you've reached the basement of your relaxation, simply rest there for as long as you like. You can drift aimlessly, if that is your desire. Or you can bring up the image or trigger for the subject you want to examine, and just allow your mind to explore it. Don't try to force questions and answers, because if you've followed the instructions, you'll be in a relatively deep state of hypnosis and your imagination will do the work.

When you know that you've gone as far as you need or want in this session, tell yourself that you're ready to emerge from hypnosis and that you can come back any time you want, and go even deeper each time. Start to count upwards, slowly, from one to three. With each number, feel yourself becoming more alert, your physical sensations returning, then your mood clearing, and finally open your eyes feeling refreshed and positive.

Always take a few moments to review what happened, and take a stretch. Don't get up too quickly, because you may have slowed your heart-rate and it might take a few moments for your circulation to come back up to speed.

Simple, isn't it! Well, it's simple for you, because you took the time and put in the work to go through the conditioning exercises. As I said at the very beginning, the more often you go into hypnosis, the easier and quicker it becomes, and the deeper you are able to descend.

It may look like there's a lot to remember, but there

really isn't. All along, I've tried to explain what to expect and what will happen, so that you have a good understanding of the hypnotic process, and that's about maintaining your confidence and belief in the efficacy. But if you want a simple step-by-step version of the instructions above, try this;

Self-hypnosis Check-List

- Get ready
- Visualise your objective.
- Say that you're ready to go into trance.
- Breathe in, breath out, say your cue word and close your eyes.
- Count down from ten to one and push out the tension so you relax completely.
- Use all your tools to go as deep as you want.
- When you're deep enough, trigger your objective image. Do what you need to do.
- Decide when you're finished, count from one up to three and emerge refreshed.
- Stretch, review, and plan your next adventure!

If you stick to this system you can't fail. It's so simple, and so logical, that you won't miss anything out or get things in the wrong order. And of course, practice makes perfect!

That's it for the tuition part. If you've followed the instructions, you will have mastered Self-hypnosis in a weekend, which is what we agreed at the start, so well done. You've been superb, and you now have a powerful skill which you can develop and polish for the rest of your life, and which will be there for you to call on whenever you feel the need.

Mission Accomplished!

And of course, if you don't feel like working too hard, and you prefer to use the recordings which you downloaded earlier, they're yours to do with what you will!

The Half-Way Point

Now, some people will decide to stop here, because this is what they wanted to achieve. However, there will be others who would like to go further, and explore some of the practical uses that this new found skill can deliver. In the second part of the book you can learn some more detailed information about hypnosis, how it works, and try some specific suggestions for common hypnosis applications. If you're leaving the train at this station, I hope you enjoyed the journey and I hope we'll meet again in a trance somewhere soon!

I'd really appreciate it if you would post a review on

your chosen bookstore if you feel you have something to say. And if you would like to keep in touch, and receive updates and new ideas, there's a Facebook Page called ricksmithhypnosis.com, where you'll always be welcome with any questions or observations.

INTRODUCTION TO SECTION TWO

Welcome back! So you decided to explore a little bit further! Hypnosis can be like that. Once you figure out how easy it is (and of course it's free too) you may find yourself drawn into the adventure that trance invites you to explore; the journey inside your own mind.

If you've followed the instructions in part one, you'll now be highly competent at the technique of hypnotising yourself. But more than that, because self-hypnosis was only a part of the instruction you received, you should also be extremely well conditioned in terms of hypnotic susceptibility.

Here's how I got hooked on hypnosis;

Hooked on Hypnosis

In 2005, I invested a huge amount of money to spend a week training with Paul McKenna, probably the most successful hypnotist on the planet, and Richard Bandler, the charismatic inventor of Neuro-Linguistic Programming.

During their course I witnessed some startling transformations; people were cured of some serious long-term issues, relieved of anxiety and phobias, and numerous bad habits and behaviours were modified and removed. I myself was the recipient of a particularly powerful change, which I'll describe in more detail another time. All of this convinced me that hypnosis really works, and I decided to explore it further. I was hooked!

The following year I took a sabbatical from my management career, and enrolled on a full-time Diploma course at the Surrey Institute of Clinical Hypnotherapy, from where I graduated with a Hypnotherapy Practitioners Diploma from the National Council of Hypnotherapy, and a Practitioners Diploma in NLP. I continued my professional development with further studies with Gerry Kine, the well-known American Hypnosis guru from the Omni Centre in Florida, as well as studying the work of the past-masters of the science, Dave Elman, Milton Erickson and Gil Boyne.

I've worked with numerous private clients since then,

in areas such as addictions, depression, and professional motivation, however I have mainly applied what I know in the business world, where I've helped busy executives to maximise their performance and career achievement.

My view of hypnosis is wholly pragmatic. It is a hugely powerful tool for good, but it needs to be quick and efficient so that people 'get it' straight away and then use it effectively. For me, it is not a new-age therapy but a natural mechanism for personal growth and attainment. We use only a fraction of our mental capacity, and hypnosis can unlock a vast array of hidden resources which we all possess, but which most of us never fully utilise.

Self-hypnosis was always something of an enigma to me. When I was studying for my diploma, my trainers included a module on how to train patients to hypnotise themselves, but I must say that it wasn't particularly convincing to me.

In the years that followed, I must have read just about every book on the subject, and I came to realise this: it's just about impossible to 'teach yourself' self-hypnosis, which is why I based this book on using pre-recorded scripts to *install* the necessary techniques, but only after spending some time conditioning you to achieve an acceptable state of trance. In my professional opinion, if you tried to learn self-hypnosis from a cold start, you would be unlikely to succeed. Using the method in this book, you are virtually guaranteed to succeed!

Now we come to the uses for self-hypnosis. Here it's important that we're honest with each other; if you are expecting to make the same kind of therapeutic break-throughs with self-hypnosis as you might with a professional hypnotherapist, we need a reality check.

Board-certified hypnotherapists train for between six months and two years to attain their professional qualifications. Once certified, most professional bodies, who regulate and supervise the hypnosis industry in the same way that doctors, dentists and nurses are overseen, require on-going programmes of 'Continuous Professional Development' and periodic supervision by a senior practitioner. In major western cities, mainstream hypnotherapy practitioners charge between $100 (£65) and $300 (£200) per session, of course part of which supports the costs of consulting rooms and the infrastructure required to operate a therapy practice.

The point of this? Well, if self-hypnosis was capable of achieving the same outcomes as professional hypnotherapy, based solely on the investment of the price of a Starbucks Latte on this book and a weekend in your back bedroom, thousands of highly qualified professionals would be out on the street!

The reality is that self-hypnosis is a very useful personal tool, but it is not the curative phenomenon of hypnotherapy. Its uses in the therapy arena are limited. Everyone's hypnosis experience is unique and personal. Once you have the skills, I would encourage experimentation to discover what works best for you. In this section of the book, we will examine the primary tool in hypnosis, *suggestion*, and ways in which it can be adapted and used to good effect in self-hypnosis.

We'll also look at some of the more common hypnotherapy interventions, namely Smoking, Weight Loss, and Stress, and discuss how self-hypnosis may be utilised as a weapon in each case.

Finally, the Resources section at the back of the book will direct you towards other places where you can obtain information, scripts and recordings should you want to go further.

7

A BRIEF HISTORY OF HYPNOSIS

What most people understand about hypnosis is largely grounded in two areas. On a personal level, you may have tried it, or know someone else who has tried it. Alternately, you'll have seen it on TV. People like Paul McKenna have really popularised hypnosis in the mainstream over the past decade by TV exposure, which has been continued by Derren Brown and others including the magician (or actually Mentalist) David Blaine.

The fundamental technique of hypnosis is 'congruent communication', particularly verbal. But the myriad of studies suggests that the process is much more complicated and sophisticated than that. The urban legend that we only use 10% or 20% of our brains is an oversimplification, but it's entirely possible that we are only 20%

competent in the use of all our brain faculties. This, of course, is the essence of training of any kind.

Hypnosis is a major part of the armoury of Witch Doctors and Shaman, as well as Faith Healers and Con Artists, who've been around since the dawn of time. It could be argued that the radicalisation of vulnerable young people by religious zealots owes a lot to hypnosis. Some schools of thought believe that part of natural evolution is the understanding of the conscious ability to tap into the subconscious rhythmic operation of the brain and the body as a whole. It seems likely that all the faculties required to enter a hypnotic state exist within a person's own mind, and that the role of the outside force such as the shaman or hypnotist is to guide the subject into accessing resources which are normally hidden, and to implant the skills to enable them to do it repetitively. In other words, you can be taught to hypnotise yourself by someone who understands the process.

In the 18th century, a physician called Franz Anton Mesmer identified the hypnotic state, and coined the term "animal magnetism", believing that it was an intangible fluid blessed with healing powers that was able to exert mutual influence between the Universe, the Earth and Animal Bodies, especially humans. He equated this fluid state as being magnetic in nature, and conducted many experiments using magnetism to demonstrate a natural or enhanced behaviour in humans and animals.

In his most famous case Mesmer treated a blind pianist and apparently restored her sight.

Unfortunately, given the political and religious environment of the day, Mesmer was labelled a fraud, and died in relative obscurity in Switzerland in 1815. However he left behind the term *mesmerised*.

Two notable British pioneers of hypnosis took the science forward in the 1800's. James Esdaile was a surgeon who used hypnotic anaesthesia successfully in hundreds of surgical operations, and in some schools of modern hypnosis the deepest state of trance is still referred to as the *Esdaile State*.

James Braid, also a physician, was particularly struck by an exhibition of mesmerism by the French expert Lafontaine, and took up intensive research thereafter. During this time there was some confusion as to whether hypnosis was a state of sleep, and Braid's induction methods were based on eye fatigue. Braid's research has only become relevant and interesting in the 20th and 21st centuries, and he did not achieve much profile in his day.

After Braid, recorded research moved to France and great strides were made in the use of hypnosis as a receptacle for suggestion techniques, and the language structures of suggestion started to develop. Sigmund Freud experimented with hypnosis for some time but eventually discarded it, probably because it did not offer him many advantages in his psychoanalytical work.

Fast-forward to the 1950s, and the era of Dave Ellman. Ellman was relatively low-key, but was widely regarded and respected in the medical and psychological communities in the USA. Ellman may be credited with having taken away a lot of the mystique surrounding hypnosis. Hypnotists of the time appear to have been somewhat anal in enhancing and dramatising the science and the therapies involved in it. There was also a great deal of fear around at the time, and the spectre of *electric shock therapy* in the mental health system frightened many people away from what they saw as *mental medicine*.

Ellman dramatically simplified the definitions of hypnosis and also the techniques used to induce it. These days confident hypnotists still employ the Ellman induction, because it enables them to take most patients into a appropriate state of trance in between five and ten minutes, rather than the thirty minute inductions favoured by the more traditional branch of science.

I use the Ellman induction almost exclusively in my own hypnotherapy practice, and it works well on almost everyone, saving a lot of time in the preamble stage and enabling more of the session to be devoted to actually solving the patient's problems.

Post flower-power, a new branch of hypnosis and psychoanalysis emerged, most notably under the leadership of Richard Bandler and John Grinder. The original concepts of Neuro Linguistic Programming (NLP) were laid out for the world in their breakthrough book "Frogs to Kings". Bandler has gone on to have a colourful career but remains at the pinnacle of the NLP movement. His description of NLP as "waking hypnosis" may be viewed as something of a paradox, since modern science confirms that all hypnosis is conducted in a waking state. Nevertheless, NLP aids the comprehension of language, and how spoken conversation can be formatted to cut through someone's critical function and exert positive influence on the subconscious and instinctive part of the personality. If you want to see a consummate NLP practitioner in action, I recommend watching one of Bill Clinton's big speeches, which can be found on Youtube. If you watch it, try to identify the small snippets of patterned language which may sound occasionally incongruous, but are carefully crafted to induce approval, compliance, or a favourable opinion in the audience.

Probably the best-known hypnotist in the UK, and now in America, is Paul McKenna. McKenna makes hypnosis look easy, but he is without doubt an outstanding exponent of the science. McKenna is not just able to hypnotise people, but he has the sixth sense which allows him to quickly empathise with the subject and, thinking on his feet, use rapid techniques to effect a change. He's rich because he's good at this. I've spent some time training with both Bandler and McKenna, separately and together, and the experience was scintillating.

Many people credit Dave Ellman with the quotation "all hypnosis is self hypnosis". The role of the hypnotist can be as a trainer. If you ever learned to ski, you can understand how it's possible to train a major new skill into someone of almost any age from a complete zero start, usually in a matter of hours.

Hypnosis is a similar process: you have all the resources to enable you to do this, but you need a guide and a trainer to explain the system by which you access them and make them work.

Then you can do Self Hypnosis.

8

HOW HYPNOSIS WORKS

As I previously mentioned, this book is written backwards. In my view, it isn't necessary for you to know how or why hypnosis works in order to experience it. In fact, given that we are trying to disable your critical faculty, it may potentially help if you don't know! So if you've followed the book in chapter sequence, you may well have mastered self-hypnosis without any information about the technical processes whatsoever.

However, if you've chosen to continue with your hypnosis education by reading the second part of the book, you're now enabled to discover some of the science and theory behind hypnosis in general, and self-hypnosis in particular.

The established theory for the function of hypnosis goes more or less like this;

Your mind, that is to say the most recognisable mani-festation of brain functionality, works on two levels, the *conscious*, and the *subconscious* (sometimes called the *unconscious*, but this is confusing).

Your *conscious* mind is paying attention most of the time. It enables you to interpret things that are going on around you, and perform conscious tasks which require some level of concentration or focus. The conscious mind also acts as a 'critical faculty' making assessments and judgements based on a combination of logic and experi-ence about all the information you receive throughout the day. It examines and decides whether the inputs are honest, reliable, safe, or useful. The conscious mind can be described as a filter, only permitting some things to penetrate your deeper brain, and outright rejecting (or at least triggering suspicion) when it encounters something which is not so clear.

Your *subconscious* mind, on the other hand, is running largely on auto-pilot. In there are stored all your learned behaviours and assumptions, about a myriad of things which are considered to be factual. For example, your subconscious mind learns how to manage your walking, talking, eating and so on, from a very early age, so you do these complex things automatically. It also seems to be in control of your memory.

Any learned behaviour is managed in the subcon-scious mind, such as driving a car, riding a bicycle, swimming, singing a song or playing an instrument. Also (and this is important) your subconscious associates emotions with experiences. Your imagination is very strong in your subconscious mind, and your imagination can simulate almost any sensation that you are capable of experiencing in 'real-life'.

How does your subconscious acquire all this information? Well, much of it arrives via your conscious mind, from your key senses – Sight, Sound, Taste, Smell, and Touch.

Based on its decision criteria, for example *safety*, your conscious mind will either admit or block a new input, which determines whether it is allowed to enter the subconscious mind, which has no such critical faculty and effectively believes everything it sees and hears. Without the filtration of your conscious mind, your subconscious would simply accept everything at face value, and you'd never be able to make a decision about anything!

Hypnosis, when done correctly, temporarily weakens the influence of the conscious mind, or even turns it off altogether. This enables information and learned behaviour to pass directly into the subconscious without any filtration.

Before we examine the value of this, it's important to eliminate the key concern that anyone would have reading this for the first time, and that is the safety aspect.

Hypnotists are always asked whether hypnosis can force people to do things against their will, and the answer is an emphatic *No!*

There is a fail-safe mechanism in your subconscious mind which is there to protect you, and simply will not allow anything dangerous to be suggested from outside which could harm you or risk any aspect of your well-being. Although hypnosis enables direct communication with the subconscious, it's not a dumb-interface, and if the instructions or suggestions don't fit within the subconscious framework of what is right and acceptable, they will not be accepted.

Now, inside your subconscious mind are all the habits and behaviours that you've acquired over your life-time, alongside all your fears and phobias. As you might say, *you are the sum of your experiences.* The problem with humans is that, along the way, some of those important things may have been corrupted by experiences, particularly when we're young and before our critical faculties are fully developed.

Take *smoking* for example; If you'd never come across smoking in your life, and at the age of thirty someone described to you a burning piece of chemically impregnated biomass which tastes dreadful, irritates your throat and chest, makes you smell terrible, costs a lot of money and will most likely deprive you of up to ten years of useful life, you wouldn't think twice about rejecting it as pointless, just as most people would reject a heroine syringe.

But a young, inexperienced mind doesn't hear these messages. A teenager hears (sees and feels) adventure, maturity, rebellion, camaraderie and a whole host of other triggers. They light a cigarette and the majority are immediately addicted for the rest of their lives.

On a deeper level, many major psychological issues which people experience in adult life can be traced back to events or circumstances in childhood. We're all shaped by the way we're nurtured, and even quite insignificant events can have a profound effect on the way our subconscious conditions us to relate to the world later on.

In recent years, there has been a spotlight on abuse, and how terribly some people behave been affected by things that occurred decades earlier. Only now are we beginning to fully understand this subject, and develop the resources within society to assist these unfortunate people.

So, when hypnosis professionals deal with cases where learned behaviour needs to be modified in order to enable someone to correct the way they relate to that aspect of their life or the outside world, the ability to speak directly to the part of the mind, the subconscious part, where such behaviours are stored and managed, is dynamite. A skilled hypnotherapist is usually able to completely fix huge long-standing issues for clients, if not in one session, usually within a matter of a few consultations.

The technique required to establish this direct communication link to the subconscious is called *hypnotic induction*. If you've worked through the exercises in this book you will have experienced induction a number of times. The hypnotism community posits that around 99% of all humans are susceptible to hypnotic induction, and those that aren't are from such distorted niches that they do not really register as a statistic; the mentally impaired, the psychopaths and sociopaths, and so on.

You may know someone who states quite categorically *"I can't be hypnotised"*. Hypnotists love to have people like that in their reclining chairs, because invariably the subject either didn't commit to accepting hypnosis in the past (which can be overcome by a skilled practitioner) or alternately they always were quite susceptible but didn't 'feel' like they were in trance the last time.

This raises an interesting subject, because the hypnosis experience is so wildly variable across the population. Some people just go out like a light, lose any awareness of their surroundings, and have no recollection afterwards. They would describe the hypnotic experience as *sleep* or *coma*, and they're invariably marvellous subjects who respond completely to any suggestion or therapy that is performed on them.

Others will say that they didn't feel anything at all, but the treatments seem to work fine on them as well. In fact, one of the 'greats' of hypnosis training dared to say that if a subject complains that he isn't going into trance, the best approach for the hypnotist is to persuade the subject to *pretend* to be hypnotised. Remarkably, the treatments appear to work equally well in this situation!

In recent years, the medical fraternity, usually society's *critical faculty*, has largely embraced hypnosis as a valid treatment for a wide variety of ailments. I suspect that if Big Pharma could find a way to make money out of hypnotherapy (so that it didn't threaten the dominance of drug therapies and hence the prescribing habits of many doctors) we would see a surge in its application for everything from pain control and anaesthesia to addiction treatment and chronic illness. These days, the National Health Service in the UK and many medical insurers across the world include hypnosis and hypnotherapy as a viable treatment option.

Anyway, that's enough from the soap-box! The fact is, hypnosis *works*. But of course you know this, now that you've learned how to do it!

Practitioner vs Self-Hypnosis

The most over-used phrase in the hypnosis industry is: *"All Hypnosis Is Self Hypnosis"*.

Almost every book on the subject opens up with that as a mantra. Whilst it may be technically true on some level, it actually doesn't really help very much. It would seem to be more valuable in the context of training yourself to understand the key differences between *Practitioner Hypnosis* and *Self-Hypnosis*, because they are significant.

Hypnosis is not the same as *Hypnotherapy*. Hypnotherapy is a hybrid term, which should be clear to you. It's therapy which is administered whilst the subject, client, or patient is in hypnosis.

Many of the therapies which are employed in this situation are very similar to protocols used by psychiatrists, counsellors, and *Cognitive Behavioural Therapists* (CBT). The advantage of these therapeutic interventions being used in a hypnosis environment is that they often work much more quickly, because they overcome patient resistance (remember the *Critical Faculty*).

Again, we'll use the smoking analogy. Later in the book, there's a transcript of probably the most common single-session Stop-Smoking script used by hypnotherapists. The success rate of hypnotherapy in smoking cessation is well-documented as being the very best method of all, statistically far more successful than Nicotine Replacement Therapy (NRT), Zyban, or any of the health education initiatives. Probably the only thing that's worked better in the last ten years was banning smoking in pubs!

Now, if you read that script to yourself, without hypnosis, it will sound bland and trite, and somewhat childish in places. You can't imagine that reading, or being read, that document would have any effect on your smoking habit.

However, when administered in the hypnosis environment, by an experienced therapist, the results are simply staggering. A substantial percentage of clients stop smoking for more than six months, and many go on to live tobacco-free for their whole lives! Intriguingly, one of the key success factors for this treatment is that *the client must pay* for the treatment. If you give it for free, success rates plummet.

So, to our comparison. I would safely say that using a conventional Stop-Smoking script in self-hypnosis will not achieve the success rate of that in the hands of a professional hypnotherapist. It's not only because of the financial aspect, but also a whole host of other human nature issues which are too expansive to explore in this book.

Self-hypnosis is not the tool for massive, instantaneous change. It's far more useful to make tactical adjustments in oneself. If something major - a key behaviour change - is required, consulting a professional hypnotherapist is the way to go.

But that's not to say that self-hypnosis can't actually work *better* in some situations. For a start, because it's free and you can use it according to your own schedule, it's a much more convenient thing to repeat over and over again, and *repetition* is a major tool in the hypnosis toolbox.

Self-hypnosis can be used very effectively to improve confidence, alleviate anxiety or performance pressure, strengthen commitment, and in all sorts of situations where the subject suffers from cognitive irrationality: that is that they know they are reacting irrationally to a situation and are capable of focusing on fact, rather than succumbing to emotion.

In the self-hypnotic trance state, the distracting triggers are suppressed, and the subject is able to zoom in on the correct way to behave, thereby strengthening the *model* which can be used to get through a difficult or challenging situation. Whilst practitioner hypnosis is highly effective in these cases, it's clearly impossible to have a hypnotherapist alongside you all the time, so the ability to quickly drop into trance and perform a predetermined routine can be highly effective in providing a quick-fix.

As we discussed earlier in the book, most people find it impossible to memorise long scripts and then carry them into the trance state, so that they can use them for *therapy*. and any self-hypnosis training which suggests otherwise is probably going to be unsuccessful for most people. So, for self-hypnosis to be an effective tool for changing yourself, it's important to use strong but simple self-suggestions which are easy to memorise and execute, once the induction has taken place.

For specifically targeted change, these suggestions should take the form of 'one-liners', which when used repetitively will lodge in the subconscious and become automatic calls to action, whenever the particular situation occurs.

In the next chapter we'll examine these techniques further and you'll learn how to write really effective mini-scripts which obey the golden rules of hypnotic suggestion.

9

SUGGESTION - THE ENGINE OF HYPNOTIC CHANGE

As we have explored in earlier chapters, the basic objective of hypnosis is to suppress the *critical faculty* (your conscious mind) in order to open a direct channel of communication to the subconscious mind. Once this is achieved, in the *trance state*, it is then practical to place good-quality behavioural information and instruction directly into the part of the brain which deals with learned behaviour. This is classified as *suggestion* and it is the foundation tool of anyone using hypnosis to effect change of any kind.

Professional hypnosis practitioners spend around ten percent of their training learning how to induce hypnosis in clients, and the other ninety percent learning the techniques of how to communicate with the client in hypnosis, based largely on *suggestion*. This is generally referred to as therapy, or the *Work*.

These strategies and techniques vary from the extraordinarily simple (*direct* suggestion) to the immensely complex, and the methods of applying suggestion can range from one-shot quick-fix techniques, to courses of therapy lasting weeks or even months.

Suggestion and Self-Hypnosis

The differences between practitioner-induced hypnotic therapy and self-hypnosis are many and varied. However, the most effective approach for us in this 'teach yourself' context is to keep things as simple as possible.

Obviously, this limits the volume of information we can include in a suggestion, not only because it heightens the risk of misinterpretation, but also because it's virtually impossible for you to memorise complex scripts and then carry them through the trance induction in order to be able to make the suggestions to yourself once you're under.

The Laws of Suggestion

- **Concentrated Attention:** Repeated attention

to a single idea will inevitably result in its realisation.

- **Law of Reverse Effect:** The harder you try to do something, the less chance that you will succeed.
- **Law of Dominant Effect:** Stronger emotions usually replace weaker ones. Facts have less power than emotions.

Whoever invented these laws gave themselves a *Get Out Of Jail Free Card*, because it should be obvious to you that not all of these conditions can exist in the same place, at the same time. So the techniques of hypnotic suggestion are loosely based on employing whichever of the 'laws' seem most applicable in any given situation!

Types of Suggestion

There are a number of different types of suggestion which can be used, such as;

- **Direct Suggestion:** The most obvious type of suggestion, which basically says *"Feel/do/say THIS and you will achieve THAT"*. Direct suggestion involves a call to action with a motivating goal attached to it. Your subconscious mind receives this type of suggestion and accepts it without resistance, because the suggestion is constructed specifically to tick all the boxes of good advice. Examples of direct suggestion might be: *"You desire those foods which help you to reach your goal"* in the case of a dieting suggestion or *"You are released from your desire to smoke"* in the case of a smoking intervention.

- **Indirect Suggestion:** These suggestions usually take the form of a question, however there is never an open-ended answer option. The indirect suggestion offers alternate answers to the question posed, both options having equally beneficial effects. In a confidence suggestion, you could use something like *"Are you gaining confidence because I suggest it or because you are learning to be more confident?"* Now you might be mildly contemptuous of the banality of such a suggestion. If someone said that to you in everyday life, you'd find it slightly bizarre. However, remember that in trance you no longer evaluate statements and questions critically, so you would tend to receive such a suggestion without any opinion on the validity of the language used, simply absorbing it as fact. In other words, *you would not be puzzled* by the use of such simplistic and illogical language whilst in trance.

- **Open Ended Suggestion:** This is a way of telling somebody in hypnosis how to feel or act, without giving them any precise position or reason to contradict the suggestion. Again, the subconscious mind will quite happily accept a suggestion such as *"You may easily find yourself reflecting on these discoveries you made in trance in the future"*. Of course, you may not, but that option is virtually eliminated by the open-ended nature of the suggestion.

- **Positive Suggestions:** Another foundation stone in our construction of suggestions for self-hypnosis will be the use of positive suggestion. Simply put, you should generally avoid the use of negative words, such as *not, no, never,* and so on, because your subconscious mind doesn't like them. Also you might miss a negative word, in which case you could accidentally implant a suggestion completely the opposite of that which was intended. There's a well known story about a hospital emergency patient whose anaesthetic failed whilst in the operating theatre. After the operation the patient lost the ability to walk, but the surgeons couldn't understand why. In the end, regression hypnotherapy was used to take the patient back and pinpoint the issue, which turned out to be that he had subconsciously heard the surgeon say *"he would never walk again"*. In actual fact, the surgeon had said *"If we hadn't got him to hospital in time, he would never walk again"*. So the story goes that the misunderstanding was corrected by the hypnotist, and the patient later regained the ability to walk. I have no idea whether this is true, but as a metaphor for positive versus negative suggestion, it is a great illustration of why hypnotic language needs to be clear and unambiguous.

- **Negative Suggestions:** Using words like *no* and *not* in suggestions can have their benefits. For example, in the hypnotic induction phase, if the hypnotist told you *"do not think about the number five"* it's probable that you would start to think about the number five. It's a useful tool if you can do it, however for the purpose of self-hypnosis, we won't be using negative suggestion.

There are numerous other types of suggestion which a hypnotist might employ, such as *Truisms, Bind and Double Bind, Permissive Suggestion* and *Compounding*.

However these are not suited to self-hypnosis, so we'll leave them on one side for now.

You may also have heard about the use of *metaphors*, in particular the Ericksonian school of hypnotherapy. This is extraordinarily powerful and effective therapy in the right hands; however it has no practical application in self-hypnosis.

Constructing Suggestions for Self-Hypnosis

At the risk of repetition, it is not practical to take complex scripts with you into the self-hypnotic state, no matter what anyone tells you. Of course you can play recorded scripts to yourself in trance, which can be very effective. But for 'pure' self-hypnosis, the best approach is to create a simple one-line suggestion which you should be easily able to recall once you have completed the induction phase for yourself. Here are the guidelines;

- **Use the Present Tense:** Statements of suggestion should be clear that you have achieved your stated objective; *"I am a non-smoker"* (the use of the negative 'non' in this context is fine because it's more or less a common noun). The future tense is a no-no: *"I will be a non-smoker"* won't work properly because it's indefinite and opens itself to interpretation by your subconscious, and the obvious question, "WHEN will I be a non-smoker?"

- **Use the Positive:** The realistic possibility that your subconscious could drop a 'not' or 'no' in a suggestion opens you up to the potential to install the exact opposite of what is intended, so steer clear of negative suggestion with self-hypnosis. An odd example not to use is *"I will not fall asleep whilst driving"*. Instead you should use *"I am awake and alert whilst driving"* which eliminates both the negative and the future tense. Remember, simple is good and less is more!

- **Don't Use 'Try':** The use of 'try' implies the potential to fail. Direct suggestion requires a binary approach, with no latitude for interpretation or excuses.

- **Consummate Visualisation:** Always visualise something that you are trying to achieve or confirm as if it is already fact, or has already happened.

S.M.A.R.T. Goal Setting

When you're preparing suggestions for use in self-hypnosis, you should focus on structuring your goals according to the following "S.M.A.R.T." acronym, which is as follows:

- *SPECIFIC:* Be precise about what it is you are trying to achieve. A single concept or idea is much easier to shape than a compound set of conditions.

- *MEASURABLE:* This could be a deadline when are going to achieve your *specific* goal, or an amount (of money perhaps) that will satisfy the criteria of 'goal achievement'.

- *ACHIEVABLE:* Here, you need to ensure there are no obstacles which might prevent you from hitting your target.

- *REALISTIC:* Hypnosis is an enabler. It is not a miracle worker, so make sure you are setting out to do something reasonable, not over-stretching yourself beyond what is realistic.

- *TIMELY:* Your plan should have a timetable which you know is achievable. If you're too aggressive with your deadline, no amount of hypnotic empowerment is going to get you there.

Using the Suggestion Phrase

If you are going to use suggestion in self-hypnosis, just follow the simple steps below;

Prepare your environment, exactly as you did in the earlier exercises. Calmly run thorough your plan (either out-loud or internally), like this:

- *In a moment, I am going to breathe in, and when I breathe out, I will take myself down into hypnosis, as I have often done before.*
- *I will take as much time as I need to become completely relaxed and ready to work on my (whatever you are planning to do).*
- *In my relaxed hypnotic state, I will suggest to myself: (insert your one-line suggestion 'script' 'x')*
- *I will take my time to thoroughly process my suggestion about 'x'*
- *When I am done, I will emerge myself to my full waking state, feeling great and ready to incorporate my new learning/behaviour/plan into my life.*

When you're ready, do it!

Writing Your Self-Suggestion

Following the rules and guidelines above, you should be able to construct a one-line suggestion script for just about anything.

Once you're in trance, and you can repeat your suggestion, you will release your full imagination which will develop the imagery or sensory experience of achieving your objective. It is a good idea to have completed the SMART exercise earlier in the chapter, so that you have a *model* of what you want to see, and how you want to feel.

The suggestion that you construct is the trigger to make all this happen, so you should make it as precise and unambiguous as you can manage. Here are some examples:

"As the days and weeks go by I am....":

- *Paying more attention to the healthy food I eat.*
- *Enjoying the freedom of living without fizzy drinks.*
- *Growing more relaxed and contented in myself.*
- *Easily able to manage the energetic requirements of my career.*
- *Filled with love and appreciation for my family/friends/etc.*

- *Excited to discover what the future holds for me, as I reach my potential in every way.*

I'm sure you get the drift by now, and you can easily construct appropriate suggestions for yourself, to suit your personal self-hypnosis objectives.

And Remember

Always accept the hypnotic experience as it comes to you. Avoid asking yourself questions such as *"am I hypnotised?"* and simply get on with the process as explained above. Remember that you are putting aside your critical faculty in order to make full use of your powerful subconscious mind.

The more questions you ask, the more you continue to engage your critical faculty, which will block your progress. The harder you try, the tougher it will be to succeed, so simply relax and let the hypnosis work in its own way. Practice makes perfect. It is not the subjective experience that matters, it is the outcome. Trust yourself and the process and it WILL work for you.

10

INSOMNIA AND SLEEP ISSUES

Sleep Problems.

Insomnia is a common complaint which often prompts people to consider hypnosis. A competent hypnosis practitioner should have been trained to work with sleep disorders, however it's rarely a single-session fix.

Sleep disorders are almost always associated with external factors – nobody simply 'can't sleep', therefore in any hypnosis approach, it's first important to run through a check-list to try to identify or eliminate potential causes.

Self-hypnosis is a well-recognised approach to insomnia, but before it can be effective, the following considerations need to be taken;

Medical Problems: Sleep disturbance caused by Apnoea or other medical problems are not well-suited to hypnosis. Apnoea is a complex subject, because the symptoms are highly distracting. Many sufferers have no idea that they are suffering sleep disturbance due to breathing obstruction, the most common form of Apnoea, but often suffer from extreme fatigue and tiredness during the day as a result. If left undiagnosed, there are a host of underlying medical issues which can develop as a result of Apnoea, so it's really important to have a doctor eliminate it as the cause, if the sleep disorder is chronic.

Psychiatric Disorders and/or Substance Dependence: Depression is a major cause of sleep disorder. Of course, if you're depressed you're probably more aware of the depression than the resultant sleeplessness. This is medical territory in the first instance, though professional hypnotherapy and it's near neighbour *Cognitive Behavioural Therapy (CBT)* are highly effective interventions for depression in many cases.

It's unlikely that hypnosis for sleep disorders will work in the case of a depressed person, who has bigger issues to confront. Drugs and alcohol are huge disrupters of sleep patterns, so here same thing applies: hypnosis is powerful, but when pitched against these chemical effects, the results are unlikely to be satisfactory.

However, lots of people suffer from sleeplessness due to one of the following *controllable* reasons;

- Cognitive over-activity or habits which are not conducive to good sleep. These people may be spending the pre-sleep hours ruminating, worrying, working, or pre-planning, and have difficulty in *switching-off* at bed-time.
- The same effect can be caused by something as innocent as reading, or watching TV just before trying to sleep.
- Nervous anxiety or tension, which can have many underlying causes.
- Unconscious fears or conflicts which affect their ability to fall or remain asleep.

Self-hypnosis, of the type you have already practiced, perhaps the *Beach* visualisation, is an excellent method of achieving deep muscle relaxation, and works well in many cases. Alongside physical relaxation, *boredom* is the weapon of choice to clear the mind of conflicting thoughts and mental interruptions. The legendary 'counting sheep' technique is highly effective, once a self-induced trance is obtained, although you may prefer to use something a little more contemporary and a little less comedic.

The objective is to concentrate the mind on something surreal or imaginary, in order to block out interfering or distracting thoughts about real life.

The simple process of focusing on total relaxation, as

you do when practising self-hypnosis, is usually enough to deal with standard sleeplessness, where there is no serious underlying stress or anxiety involved. Now that you're trained in hypnosis and the use of your imagination, you can easily construct a surreal mental environment to use at bed-time.

Sleep Hygiene

However, before attempting any of this, there are some important practical steps which you should take, to remove and eliminate any external factors which may be contributing to your sleep problems. Many of these sound obvious or even silly, but they've been proven to work over many thousands of interventions, so don't dismiss them until you've tried them;

- Only sleep (or have sex) in bed, in your bedroom. Don't do anything else in that room (apart from maybe sorting gout your wardrobe!). Don't read in bed, don't watch TV or listen to the radio or music. Your bedroom is *only* for sleeping, so that is all you should be doing in there. If you decide, once you are in your bedroom, that you want to do any of these other things, you should immediately get up and go to another room.

- If you're still awake half an hour after retiring, you should get up, go to another room, and do something useful for a short time. Many people find cleaning works for them. After a further thirty minutes, you should try to sleep again.
- Is your bedroom chaotic? Sanitising the environment is important. Remove any clutter, obstructions, or unrelated items. Tidy up if necessary. It's important that you regard your bedroom as a place of peace and good order, or it will have a derogatory effect on your state of relaxation.
- If sounds are a problem, consider the use of airline ear-plugs. They don't work for everyone (some people are disturbed by the sound of their own breathing) but if you're a light sleeper and you have noisy neighbours, they will help you to remain undisturbed.
- Only go to bed when you're tired. Never take naps during the daytime. Do not sleep anywhere else in the house (on the couch, for example).
- Set your wake-up alarm for the same time every day, even the weekends. Routine is really important.
- Warm milky drinks and small carbohydrate

snacks, such as unsweetened biscuits, just before bed time can raise serotonin levels, which encourage deeper sleep. But avoid anything else, particularly sugary snacks.

- A hot bath can help. By artificially raising your body temperature, you kick-start accelerated cooling afterwards. Cooling is an important component of falling asleep.

- Darkness is very important. Your circadian rhythm, the internal clock which tells you when you should be sleeping, relies on Melatonin to keep good time. Melatonin production is suppressed by light (especially blue light from TV's, phones and computers. Over 50's naturally suffer from depleted melatonin; consult your doctor, who may prescribe melatonin supplementation, which is highly beneficial for your overall health, not just your sleep patterns.

- If you can't black out your bedroom, get a sleep mask. The airline masks are rubbish because they press on your eyes. I use a Mindfold mask, which has foam around the eyes so the mask doesn't touch them. I first got it for overnight flights, but now I wear it every night, especially in the summer when the sun comes up at 4.30am!

Setting up for sleep is like setting up to do self-hypnosis. If the environment isn't right, any issues will be magnified, and distractions will interfere with your regular sleep pattern.

If you use self-hypnosis to relax yourself, and you want a simple one-line suggestion to repeat to yourself once you are in trance, try something like:

> *"I may descend into deep sleep soon or a little later, and good sleep is deeply refreshing for my body and mind"*

Remember to keep the wording positive, and use (incontrovertible) alternatives.

One approach that works well with a little practice is this:

- Prepare your bedroom as above.
- Throughly cleanse, bathe, and even (men) shave, and make yourself feel 'nice'.
- Sit quietly for a few moments and 'set aside' any issues or concerns that may be troubling you. You're going to sleep now, to re-charge your energy so you can face tomorrow positively.
- Focus on something that you'd like to explore

with visualisation. Maybe something real that's potentially attainable and which would make you happy. You're going to use this imagery and the feelings that come with it in a moment.

- Darken the room and settle in bed. The day is officially over for you.
- Remind yourself of your visualisation plan.
- Focus on progressively relaxing your body, from the feet up. Go painstakingly through every bone and joint, ensuring that it's as relaxed as possible, before moving upwards to the next.
- If you're still awake by the time your reach your head, execute your self-hypnosis induction using your cue word.
- Immerse yourself in your fantasy, and enjoy how it feels.

If you'd like some more help with your sleep issues, my new hypnosis audio course *Sleep Fast, Sleep Deep, Sleep Now* is available to download from my website at ricksmithhypnosis.com.

The book includes over five hours of specially recorded audio downloads.

THE ALL-NEW HYPNOSIS
APPROACH TO INSOMNIA

SLEEP FAST
SLEEP DEEP
SLEEP NOW

Rick Smith HPD DHyp

11

STRESS, PANIC, AND ANXIETY

In the first section of this book, you learned how to place yourself into hypnosis, firstly by allowing a hypnotist's spoken script to guide and condition you, and then by using the same techniques on your own. So, now that you have mastered the techniques, what are you going to do with them?

Relaxation and Stress Reduction

In the self-hypnosis context, these are versions of the same thing. The word *Relax* implies that you are changing your state of being from one of tension (which might be entirely healthy tension) to one of no-tension.

Though most people would logically associate relaxation with a physical manifestation, it's reasonable to assume that if you can relax physically it will necessarily follow that you can relax mentally too. If this sounds familiar, it should, because it's the opening salvo in the standard hypnotic induction.

Stress is a more heightened state of 'non-relaxation' which is generally viewed as a negative or harmful state. People who encounter stress can often become strangely addicted to it. If you're in a state of stress - which may engender feelings of anxiety or panic - you are generally focussed in on activity to find a solution to the stress itself, rather than an analysis of the underlying causes or triggers.

So the stress state can provide a distraction which stops you thinking about the actual issues, and concentrates all your physical and mental resources on navigating the stress itself.

However there is nothing good about stress. It's not a mental process, but a whole-body experience which is driven and sustained by chemical imbalance.

Adrenaline, Cortisol, Norepinephrine

The three key chemicals in the stress process are Adrenaline (Epinephrine), Cortisol, and Norepinephrine

All of these are produced by the adrenal gland, located adjacent to your kidneys, although norepinephrine is also produced in parts of the brain, possibly as a back-up if the adrenal gland is malfunctioning, which can have a wide variety of causes.

Simply put, adrenaline and norepinephrine are responsible for short-term elevations in stress as in the *fight-or-flight* response, whereas cortisol over-production is the end result of a longer and more complex process, and is responsible for chronic stress disorders.

Everyone's heard about fight or flight, when the body adjusts to a threatening situation by focusing its resources on the essential survival functions, such as sight and hearing, muscle reaction, and suppression of fear. That's usually adrenaline at work, and in small doses it can be quite beneficial. Energy bursts, pain suppression, and a host of other 'super-powers' can be temporarily effected by adrenaline, which is essentially triggered by stressful situations as they occur.

Cortisol is a steroid hormone and is one of the most important chemicals that the body produces. It too is manufactured in your adrenal gland, and is essential for balancing bodily systems such as blood pressure, glucose metabolism, insulin levels, and inflammatory response. The release of cortisol into your bloodstream is part of your primordial response system.

Heightened stress over long periods will ultimately shorten your life-span. In ancient times the constant struggle for survival meant that cortisol and stress, whilst useful as a protection mechanism, did not mitigate for longevity. For our cave-dwelling ancestors this was not such a problem, because there were a million other things out there that would kill them before they hit thirty.

But these days, since we have medical science to keep us going well into our seventies or eighties, the cortisol/stress response is intrusive and dangerous, since it has not evolved with modern life.

So, if cortisol and stress are essentially unavoidable, unless you're one of those fortunate people who can self-regulate, you need a strategy to deal with stress which suppresses the damage that it can do to your body if it is allowed to remain unchecked, the condition known as *chronic stress.*

The best way to approach this is to sharpen your *relaxation response,* so that you can come off the stress plateau quickly, thereby reducing your cortisol levels to normal. If you don't pay attention to this, over time a surfeit of cortisol can contribute to some or all of the following debilitating and often irreversible physical ailments;

- Hypothyroidism
- Blood sugar problems, leading to hyperglycaemia and diabetes
- Leaching bone density, leading to osteoarthritis

- Elevated blood pressure, heightening stroke and cardiac injury risk
- Heightened fat retention, a component of the dangerous *metabolic syndrome*

Training your relaxation response is a very effective way to deal with stress, and self-hypnosis is one of the key weapons in your armoury.

The self-hypnosis technique for stress control is quite simple. It's based on taking control of your key functions, such as breathing, muscle tension, and heart-rate. If you have followed the earlier exercises, particularly the *Beach* exercise, you already have the necessary skills to do this.

However, knowing how to do something, particularly in a super-distracted state such that stress engenders, is not the same as doing it. For this to work, you actually have to recognise the stress symptoms as they arise, and make a long-term commitment to using a standard intervention each time. In addition, there are some practical steps you can take in your everyday life which will lessen the risk of stress symptoms occurring, such as:

- *Caffeine:* everyone knows that coffee is a strong stimulant. It also has some beneficial health effects, and it's a really nice and sociable drink, so nobody's advocating that you give up coffee. However, if you are drinking more than one or two cups in the morning, you're probably going to be wired by lunchtime. In susceptible people this will lower the bar considerably, meaning that even relatively innocuous triggers can provoke anxiety and stress reactions. Stress accompanied by caffeine overdose is really tricky to counteract with hypnosis or relaxation techniques, because instead of managing your internal body systems to reduce cortisol production, you are fighting against an artificial stimulant.

- *Smoking:* Despite what you may think about smoking as a relaxation aid, nicotine is a powerful stimulant. Luckily it is a short-term chemical, and disperses quickly. The reason people regard smoking as a relaxation aid is because the ritual of smoking when you feel tense is a 'self-reward' action. How you perceive smoking actually has a greater effect on your mentality than the chemical action of the smoking itself. But you can be sure that if you're in a state of chronic stress, the ritual of smoking will only relieve you for as long as it allows you to change your situation, such as stepping outside the building. The nicotine in the cigarette smoke will actually work against you, and prolong the underlying stress state.

It's arguable that those heavy smokers who claim that smoking actually helps them de-stress are actually perpetuating their own stress conditions, but they've been doing it for so long that they actually believe their own propaganda.

- *Alcohol Misuse:* Whilst it is true that alcohol is essentially a depressant, the incumbent ritual and social effects of drinking can have a profound effect on general mental health, and particularly stress. While a cocktail or a beer after work might help you relax, in the long run it can contribute to feelings of depression and anxiety, making stress harder to deal with. This is because regular, heavy drinking interferes with neurotransmitters in our brains that are needed for good mental health. Drinking narrows your situational perception, so if you are prone to anxiety and notice something that could be interpreted as threatening in the environment, you'll tend to hone in on that and miss the other less threatening or neutral information which ordinarily would give you a balanced view of a situation. This is one of the reasons why fights break out in pubs!

Stress Reduction Technique

The technique I recommend for dealing quickly with stressful situations comes in two forms; firstly, a technique that you practice daily (or even more often) in order to instil a long-term suppression of the chronic stress symptoms. Secondly, a quick-fix you can use anywhere when you feel the stress rising. These two interventions work well together, sort of like a 'parent and child' set-up.

Like any self-administered therapy, this will only work if you make a solid commitment to sticking at it. Human nature being what it is, we expect instant results. But stress is a complicated thing, which has both physical and psychological components. It helps to name it; *Stress* is the enemy, and once you accept that it is the focus of your attention, you will be able to deal with it in an unambiguous way.

The commitment model has three stages;

- Understanding and acknowledging that you are susceptible to stress.
- Acknowledging the dangers of stress, to both your health and your happiness (and others around you)
- Activating a personal plan to combat stress, and eliminating it from your life.

Think through these three stages in order, and when you're ready to get to work on it, do a simple self-hypnosis session using the following suggestion, once you're in trance:

> *"My life is better in every way once I leave stress behind me"*

That post-hypnotic self-suggestion will trigger a visualisation (or kinaesthetic) process which will enable you to experience the benefits of dispensing with stress. Once you've made the suggestion, dwell in your trance for as long as it takes to fully appreciate the positive change that will come about, once you master your stress-elimination strategy.

Once this commitment is fixed in your mind, there's no turning back. Nothing good can come of holding onto stress in your life, so why would you want to keep it?

Armed with that commitment, here are your exercises:

Your Daily Exercise

It's important to set up a routine to complete this short exercise each day. If you're home-based, try to find a twenty minute slot as early in the day as possible when you have no other pressing responsibilities. If you work in an office, or any other external location, allocate a time-slot (perhaps during your lunch-break) when you can shut yourself away and do the exercise.

Set yourself up in your normal self-hypnosis environment, run through your checklist, and start your self-induction.

Once you've achieved a suitable level of trance, that is to say that you recognise that you're calm, relaxed, and completely inwardly-focused, use the following self-suggestion:

> *"I control my stress, it does not control me. I am in charge, I am the boss. And any time I feel stress coming, I will put myself into neutral and the stress will be gone"*

The Gear-Shift Visualisation

The visualisation to use here is that of a car's gearstick-shift, on your left side or your right side (depending on which side of the road you drive in your country). Visualise grasping the stick-shift knob, exactly as you would when driving, and slide it smoothly backwards into the neutral position, then waggle it from side-to-side, which is only possible in neutral.

This symbolises disengagement, and if you practice it

repeatedly in self-hypnosis it will become a habit which you can then use out in the real world.

Whilst in trance, *feel how it feels* to slip that gear-shift into neutral, and let all the tensions dissipate from your body and mind. You should keep practicing this visualisation. You can even physically move your hand if that helps you to experience it.

Remember, we are implanting new learned behaviour into your subconscious mind, so repetition is a very effective technique to ensure that it is thoroughly embedded. *Good habits replacing bad ones.*

When you've mastered slipping into neutral, emerge yourself from your trance, feeling great and positive.

Using Neutral Gear in Real Life

Now you've embedded this technique, you have your weapon to use whenever you feel stress rising in you. It's really that simple. The moment you feel anything disturbing coming along, you will recognise it as stress because you named it, and committed to eliminate it from your life.

Breathe in, breathe out, and use your gear shift. Really use your hand to slip the stick backwards into neutral, and waggle it from side to side a couple of times. You have put yourself into neutral. The more you use this technique, the more effective it will be, and you will become very aware of how well it works. Come to rely on it, even become addicted to it. Once you've mastered it, you'll be amazed at how easy it is to remain calm, even in the face of tremendously stressful situations.

Remember; *the situation may be outside your control, but your reaction to it is entirely within your control.*

You now have a technique that you have taught yourself, which you can use anywhere, anytime, to accelerate your relaxation response. By using the 'neutral shift' technique, you deal with the onset of stress during the short-term *adrenaline* stage, and that will interfere with the longer chain-reaction of the *cortisol* stage, thereby negating the risk of chronic stress, the *silent killer.*

This is a tactical intervention for dealing with stress as it arises. As you become calmer, as a result of mastering situations which would previously have caused you panic or anxiety, you may begin to find that the world slows down, and that you have a better overall set of coping mechanisms.

We're here to learn about self-hypnosis, but on a general coaching point I recommend that as you clear the head-space to consider the way you manage your life more strategically, you might examine ways of reducing chaos in your life. The better organised you can become, the fewer unexpected situations will arise for you, and you'll soon begin to see that much of the stress we all encounter in our daily lives is directly or indirectly of our own making.

You can discover audio hypnosis programs from Anxiety, Stress, and other related challenges, on my website ricksmithhypnosis.com

12

HYPNOSIS AND SMOKING

If you know someone who has been to see a hypnosis practitioner, the chances are that it was for help to quit smoking. Apart from a small group of highly specialised practitioners, a significant percentage of general hypnosis is about "Smoking Cessation", which is the industry standard term for a single session hypnosis treatment intended to make the subject stop smoking there and then.

Hypnosis' Greatest Success Story

This type of treatment is widely acclaimed for its efficacy, and the figures would tend to support the assertion that it outstrips virtually all other forms of stop-smoking interventions by a significant margin. So, in simple terms, it works pretty well.

Just about all professional hypnosis practitioners can do this treatment, and most use a single-session script which focuses on more or less the same thing, which is a dramatic visualisation of the damage and pointlessness of smoking, leading into a highly positive reinforcement of how powerful the subject is going to be in dealing with their future, which is going to be long and healthy.

It's a one-size-fits-all approach, and for those subjects who tick most of the boxes for susceptibility, it will stop them smoking. For some it lasts a few days or weeks, and for others it lasts their whole life. Obviously, the professionalism with which the hypnotist delivers the induction and the scripted intervention is a key factor in the success rate. However, this is not the whole story.

Why It Works So Well

Committing a substantial amount of money to such a treatment – around £150 - £200 in the UK – although easily justified in terms of money saved on cigarettes, means that most subjects view this visit to the hypnotist as a potentially life-changing event, and this enables them to build up their commitment level well in advance of the actual treatment. Smart hypnotherapists will never 'fit-in' a smoking patient the next day. The system usually works so much better if there are three or four days between the booking and the session, because this puts the forthcoming *stop-smoking event* fully front-and-centre in the mind of the client.

They start to make plans about how it might be before and after. Sure, some find it all too daunting and cancel the appointment, but this is likely to be far less of a failure rate than if the treatment is hurried. They tell their friends and relatives that they are going for the treatment, and this creates a commitment and obligation. After all, everybody wants their friends and relatives to quit smoking; that's a given. So the more people they tell, and the closer they get, not only does it make it more difficult to cancel, but it also builds a willingness to succeed, so that nobody feels let down or that they are a failure.

Then there's the *line of commitment*, which I've mentioned elsewhere in this book. Many smokers are quite capable of quitting first thing on a Monday morning, or on the first of the month, or New Years Day.

It's simple, you just stop.

But it's also easy, when the first cravings become intrusive, to smoke again, giving yourself the argument that *"I'll try again next week"*. However, as we just established, if you book with a hypnosis practitioner, especially if you pre-pay a deposit, you're drawing a huge line of commitment for yourself, which once you cross it will put a multitude of forces in play to prevent you from slipping backwards in the short term.

And within a few days of quitting, all the physical withdrawal symptoms are gone, so if you can just get through the early stage (when the lingering effect of the hypnosis is at its most potent) the physical pressures are greatly diminished, which removes a very large failure factor from the overall process.

Next, you might think that all the hypnotist does is induce a trance, deliver a script, emerge the client, take the money and that's the end of it. However, the process also involves a finely tuned pre-talk phase, which involves the hypnotist interviewing the client in questionnaire form, and explaining some important technical and physiological facts about smoking. The questionnaire part is interesting because the hypnotist really doesn't need to know much about a client in order to deliver the smoking intervention, since just about everyone smokes for the same reasons.

However, it's a really excellent way of getting the client to focus in on the elements of their habit, and examining the dynamics of why they started smoking, why it's dumb, and why they will stop. The skill and technique which the hypnotist uses in this pre-talk phase will have a great bearing on the success of the overall intervention.

And last but by no means least there is the money.

People assign value to professional services based on how much they pay, rather than how much they'll save as a result. So, even though it's easy to equate the cost of the treatment to (say) thirty days of average cigarette expenditure, that doesn't really work for most people.

However, if you equate £150 to ninety minutes of 'specialist service', when compared to your own hourly professional rate, it feels like something pretty special, which serves to reinforce the belief that it will work. Alongside this is the 'Wisdom of Crowds' weapon of influence (read Robert Cialdini for more on this) which also supports a belief system that *"if it worked so often for others, it's going to work for me"*.

All of these elements contribute to the efficacy of the smoking cessation hypnosis system.

Smoking and Self-Hypnosis

So, if we look at self-hypnosis in the same context, how effective is it likely to be?

Well. It's awfully difficult, even in hypnosis, to convince yourself of a whole new behavioural system which is at odds with the smoking habit you may have perfected over many years. Also, you aren't paying for it (apart from the tiny sum you may have invested in this book). The level of commitment to stop smoking may be strong, but the actions associated with doing it yourself are small, in comparison to the practitioner route.

So, in summary, if we try to emulate the hypnosis practitioner intervention in a self-hypnosis context, it's unlikely to be very effective for most people.

That's why I would highly recommend that if you're serious about quitting, you should find a reputable hypnotherapist (all the professional bodies have accreditation lists online), invest the money, and do it properly. Your chances of success are good, and if you've followed the exercises in this book you'll already be well conditioned to achieve a good level of trance, and this will make the treatment much more effective than someone going into hypnosis from cold.

However, that is not to say that self-hypnosis can't be an extremely useful weapon in stopping smoking if it's applied in a different way.

A major factor in changing behaviour is *positive reinforcement*, which is something that can be very effectively achieved in self-hypnosis. Another benefit of having developed the ability to drop quickly into trance is that you can easily distract yourself and focus on a committed course of action, for example, if having recently quit smoking you have an onset of cravings to smoke.

To harness these tools, the ideal process is to make the decision to quit smoking, do it naturally – 'cold turkey' if you like - then apply self-hypnosis tactically to help you through the first few days, and then strategically for the longer term.

First, here are some facts which should really help you with your decision to stop;

Smoking Key Facts:

- On average, smokers die ten years younger than non-smokers. Evidence suggests that people who quit before they're forty get nine of those ten years back, and in your thirties you can completely reverse the damage so that it has no effect for most people. Whatever your age, you will definitely regain years of useful life, once you stop smoking.
- Every time you smoke, your heart rate, blood pressure, and risk of stroke increase. The additional adrenalin production can be a contributory factor to diabetes, and most smokers' resting heart rate is 15-20 beats above normal.
- In the UK alone, over one hundred people each day die an early death through smoking. Doctors attribute in excess of 150,000 heart attacks a year to smoking.

- A smoker is nine times more likely to contract a life threatening cancer than a non-smoker.

- The heart works so much harder for a smoker, beating up to 10,000 extra beats every single day as it struggles to combat the effects of smoking chemical by-products sticking to the fatty deposits in your arteries, restricting, clogging, closing up those arteries, increasing blood pressure as it strives to deliver enough oxygenated blood so necessary for the function of the vital organs of your body, the muscles, the brain.

- Each time you take cigarette smoke into your lungs, you introduce into your body in excess of four thousand different chemical compounds; many of them deadly poisons; none of them in any way beneficial. Your body reacts to these lethal poisons in the same way as when subjected to sheer terror, the automatic response we know as fight or flight is activated, adrenaline production is elevated, respiration increases, blood pressure increases, as the body prepares to fight or to run away from danger. Nicotine, tar, ammonia, benzopyrene, carbon monoxide, arsenic, cyanide (to name just a few) are absorbed into the tissues of your body.

- Each smoker inhales just 15% of the smoke from their own cigarette; the remainder goes directly into the atmosphere that we all have to breathe. Those whom you love and care for most also breathe in the smoky poisoned air that the smokers have created.

I don't think there's anyone on the planet who can truly say that they're glad they started smoking. Likewise, even if smokers are in denial (most are), pretty much all of them would love to quit. Unfortunately, what prevents many from ever trying is the fear of how they will cope once smoking is not an available option for them. The familiar smoke-breaks, the cigarette after a meal or with a drink. The social aspects of smoking can be very compelling, and that's why it can be difficult to overcome the *fear of quitting.*

But if you can get your head around it, it's actually really simple;

    You stop. You recover. You live longer.

I said in the beginning that I don't advocate self-hypnosis alone as a viable method of stopping smoking. If it was that simple, the hypnotherapist industry would die overnight! If you're serious, you should consult a professional hypnotherapist, because that's the most effective way, for all the reasons mentioned above.

Notwithstanding, if you want to try quitting 'cold-turkey', or with the aid of nicotine replacement therapy (NRT), you can employ self-hypnosis as a reinforcement or support mechanism to help you maintain your motivation. Simply use your normal self-hypnosis routine, and utilise the following self-suggestion once you're in trance:

> *"Every day my life improves because I am free of smoking"*

See what kind of visualisation you can conjure up when you use that phrase.

The Pull of Addiction

The longer term issue with any kind of smoking intervention is this; for the first few days or weeks, you feel consciously better in terms of your health. Your sleeping patterns improve, your appetite returns, your fitness, especially if you like gym or sport, rapidly increases.

However, after a while this new state of health becomes your 'norm' and you forget all the dreadful and harmful aspects of smoking. That's the danger zone, because it's often the case that people think: *"I've beaten the addiction, so if I could just have one cigarette I would really enjoy it and that would be it".*

It doesn't work. If you try that you will probably end up smoking again at the same rate or even worse than before you stopped. Like an alcoholic, a smoker is always an addict in some part of their DNA, so when you stop, you must stop forever. That's the mindset you must adopt: *"I will never ever smoke again".*

Any time you sense the craving, just drop yourself into trance and remind yourself how well you've done, how proud you are of your own achievements, how much longer you are going to live, or whatever was the primary motivator for you to stop in the first place.

Aids and Alternatives

If you have a smartphone, download an app called 'Quitter'. You simply enter the date you quit, and the amount you used to smoke, and this app will always be there to remind you about how well you've done, how long it's been, and most importantly how much money you saved. If you live in the UK or the USA, cigarettes are so expensive these days that you'll soon see the hundreds and thousands of pounds or dollars mount up, which is a tremendous incentive to keep going.

Books & CD's

There are two Self-Help books that have a high success rate, if visiting a hypnotherapist is out of your reach, for whatever reason. Buy either or both of these:

- *Quit smoking Today Without Gaining Weight* – Paul McKenna (includes CD)
- *Allen Carr's Easy Way To Stop Smoking* – Allen Carr

These will get you started once you've made the decision to quit, then the little reinforcement routines you can do in your own self-hypnosis will keep you strong, whilst you eliminate smoking from your life.

I have a complete stop-smoking program, including six days of support (20 sessions) available on my website at ricksmithhypnosis.com

Electronic Cigarettes

In the last couple of years, electronic cigarettes - *e-cigs* - have gained tremendous popularity. There's still some opposition to this blatant form of NRT, because it mimics all the habitual aspects of real smoking and maintains the smoker's dependence on nicotine.

However, as a pragmatist, I can't see a whole lot wrong

with this strategy (I used it myself) because it gets rid of the most harmful aspects of smoking without imposing any kind of withdrawal, the main reason why people fail. It costs around 20% of the cost of real cigarettes.

There's a great deal of debate about the safety of e-cigs. I don't know any more than anyone else about this, but I do know that there's a lot of politics in play, as Big Tobacco and Big Pharma wrestle for control of the burgeoning new market.

So, I offer you this 2015 quote from the government body Public Health England:

> *"the current best estimate is that e-cigarettes are around 95% less harmful than smoking."*

Whatever your chosen course, I wish you the best of luck with stopping smoking. It is a profound life-changing experience for most people, and deserves to be taken very seriously. Sorry to bore you, but I really recommend you seek out a reputable Hypnotherapist, condition yourself with self-hypnosis before you go, and really commit to the process. You will probably save your own life!

Typical Hypnotherapist Stop-Smoking Script (for information only)

Now as you relax, drifting deeper with every word I speak, the first thing I would like you to know is how much I appreciate and admire you for the decision you have made to get rid once and for all of this foul habit.

Now you have those physical signs that allow you to know that you have moved from one conscious state to another in a calm and confident way. In this calm and confident state you can offer yourself generous portions of self confidence... large helpings of self-esteem, breathing out self-doubt as you relax even deeper and continue to enjoy the journey towards your goal.

Your conscious mind is fully aware of all the dangers to health and life that are the legacy of tobacco; after all there are enough warnings on TV and in the press for all to see; there are even warnings on the packets that you buy... and what about the obscene waste of hard-earned cash that smoking signifies? Perhaps here, now, it is worthwhile to review with your subconscious mind the damage that is inflicted by you on your body each time you light up a cigarette.

The facts are these... in this country alone, over 100 people each day die an early death through smoking. Doctors attribute in excess if 150,000 heart attacks a year to smoking, and although cancer would appear to be the most obvious health hazard, and it is true that a smoker is 9 times more likely to contract a life threatening cancer than a non-smoker, it can be so easy to say "it won't happen to me. Cancer happens to other people". Perhaps then it is right that we now consider some of the other ways in which smoking can damage your health and even threaten your life itself.

First there is the heart. The heart works so much harder for a smoker, beating up to 10,000 extra beats every single day as it struggles to combat the effects of nicotine by- products sticking to the fatty deposits in your arteries, restricting, clogging, closing up those arteries, increasing blood pressure as it strives to deliver enough oxygenated blood so necessary for the function of the vital organs of your body, the muscles, the brain.

Some people believe that a cigarette helps them to relax... now I invite your subconscious mind to review and question that statement. In the light of the knowledge that, in addition to the fact that your heart is working so much harder, each time you take cigarette smoke into your lungs you introduce into your body in excess of 4000 different chemical compounds, many of them deadly poisons, none of them in any way beneficial. Your body reacts to these lethal poisons in the same way as when subjected to sheer terror, the automatic response we know as "fight or flight" is activated, adrenaline production is elevated, respiration increases, blood pressure increases, as the body prepares to fight, or to run away from danger. Nicotine, tar, ammonia, benzopyrene, carbon monoxide, arsenic, cyanide, to name just a few, and what about the chemical fertilisers and insecticides that are sprayed on growing tobacco leaves, remaining to be included in cigarettes, now absorbed in the tissues of your body.

Does this sound like relaxation? You know the truth, and this truth now becomes deeply embedded in the subconscious of your mind, never to be denied.

As your heart works harder, your lungs strive to perform their essential function. The inside of your lungs and airways are covered in tiny hair-like projections and these become coated with sticky thick tar... they lie flat against the walls of the airways, now unable to perform their functions of preventing infectious matter from entering into the small air spaces where oxygenation of the blood takes place. The lungs become less efficient as they clog with filth... the mucus lining of the lungs becomes weakened and the whole body is starved of oxygen. Deprivation of oxygen to the brain can mean that the clear thinking ability of a smoker is diminished by up to a quarter. Smoking impairs your ability to concentrate... It fogs your mind... clouds your judgement... but I don't want you to think about that too much.

Pulmonary emphysema, chronic bronchitis, lung cancer, asthma, the coughs and the colds, so frequent and so difficult to shake off, the breathlessness that obliges you to use the lift when it would be so easy to use the stairs. The coughing, the mucus, the vile taste when you wake up in the morning,, the awful smell that others notice that is an integral part of you. You think it comes from your clothes but I am here to tell you that it mainly comes from the pores of your skin, and is so offensive to those who object to your vile and antisocial habit of smoking. You are intensely aware that you are not welcome in many public places... theatres, pubs, restaurants... at work... at play... you indulge your habit out of sight, in secret, ashamed and guilty. The taste and the smell you chose for so long to ignore is now strong... and from this moment forward you are reminded, constantly, powerfully, in a manner which cannot be ignored each time that you are reminded of cigarettes.

Tissue which does not receive enough oxygen will die, as arteries becomes constricted and blocked... arteriosclerosis becomes a word with particular meaning for you, as, deprived of oxygen... part of you dies.... Your skin wrinkles, you age prematurely. You're teeth become stained and your gums become problematic as smoking causes bone to erode. Ask yourself right now, is this for you?

Heart disease, stroke, cancer of the liver, the throat, the pancreas, the kidneys, of the tongue. Skin cancer, ulcers, the list is endless and unforgiving, as the hospitals and modern medicine struggle to cope with the self imposed destruction of those who are unwilling to accept the responsibility for their own life, their own health and happiness, to protect and respect the miracle of their own body.

Each smoker inhales just 15% of the smoke from their own cigarette; the remainder goes directly into the atmosphere that we all have to breathe. Those whom you love and care for most, also breathe in the smoky poisoned air that the smokers have created. Perhaps you can agree with me that one very good reason for quitting this disgusting habit is, that through your excellent example, you may influence someone younger against taking up the habit. Just think of how much you could achieve, if just one young person was prevented from taking up the smoking habit. Think of all the misery and pain that could be prevented if that costly and disgusting mistake could be avoided.

Now I want you to imagine an ashtray... it's your ashtray... the ashtray contains the entire residue from the cigarettes that you have smoked in the last week. I want you to feel the weight in your hand. Now, bring the ashtray towards your nose... smell the ashtray. Take a deep breath of that stale foul-smelling stench. Look at the contents, the remnants of cigarettes. The butts, and the ash. Now I want you to do something you would never normally do. I want you to dip your hand in and take a good handful of the contents and start to put it into your mouth. Feel the butts and the ash washing over your tongue, the bits of ash between your teeth, and as you chew you can taste the foulness, the disgusting chemicals that you have been putting into your body for years. Now I want you to swallow, yes swallow that foul concoction... that's it... swallow it down, feel it sliding down your throat... and now I want you to do something that you would NEVER do. I want you to stick out your tongue and lick the ashtray clean. Imagine that foul black scum clogging the pores of your tongue. Feel the *gritty texture and imagine that acrid taste on your tongue, and from this day forwards, anytime you think of cigarettes or smoking, your subconscious will remind you in a manner which cannot be denied or ignored of the vile odour and disgusting taste.*

Well done. You're doing great.

Now... in a moment |I'll ask you to take a deep breath, and then as you release all the air from your lungs, relax and go deeper... Take the breath, long and deep, that's good. And exhale, and go deeper.(DONE) Now I want you to imagine a time in the future when you are in a room, and all around you are those you love and care for, and who love and care for you... all who celebrate your decision to get rid of smoking and take responsibility for your own health, your own life.

As you go deeper now, see them all before you, gathered here as you listen to the sound of my voice and the truth that is so important to you now. They're all here, they have come from far and near to be with you. They are here because they know that you have something important to tell them......... a dreadful truth... Your doctor has told you that you have contracted cancer and that you have only a short time to live. Soon you will be gone... you will be dead before your time... all because you ignored all the good advice, the wishes of those who wanted so much for you to get rid of smoking... you made the choice... a choice to die... and soon you will not be there for those who rely on you to be a part of their life and happiness.

You refused to accept the responsibility for your own

health and for your own life, and now the immune system that you have relied on without consideration for so long to repair the ravages you have inflicted upon your own body has given up, overwhelmed, defeated. Now you will die before your time and you realise that this room you are in is in a hospital and for a moment you float up and out of your body and look down on yourself, frail and pale, with a respirator mask over your mouth and tubes up your nose, and you are in a wheelchair because you no longer have the strength to move around or breath for yourself, and you must tell all those friends and relations that terrible truth.... And tell them why.... And tell them who is responsible. Go ahead now and as you tell them, see their faces, see the smiles change to disbelief, the shock, the horror, then the anger, the grief. How do you feel?

An insidious habit has destroyed everything.... Your health, your life, wasted enormous amounts of money, filling the banks of those fat-cat tobacco companies who benefit without conscience or regard for the misery they distribute, selling in attractive packaging what you now know to be lethal poison.

Now feel the guilt... the guilt that for so long has been repressed and ignored each time you lit up a cigarette. Now feel it strongly, so strong and powerful, the feeling of shame when sneaking away to indulge in that filthy destructive habit away from family, friends and colleagues who are offended by it.

See ashtrays overflowing with stale and stinking cigarette butts, burnt holes in furnishing and clothes, stained paintwork and ceilings, brown and dingy, intensely aware now of the smell that lingers and of that taste that disgusts you now and each time you are reminded of cigarettes. And now remind yourself of the commitment that you have made today, your promise to yourself, that commitment now growing strong and powerful... intense now...your desire to pollute your mouth, your body, has gone completely.... And your subconscious mind helps you now with new and powerful responses and your desire to smoke has gone... vanished completely, replaced with feelings of justifiable pride and deep personal satisfaction.... Feelings of real and significant accomplishment.

Each day you feel stronger... more alive... your confidence and good feelings about yourself expand and grow... become powerful... no longer do you offend those around you with stinking, tobacco-laden breath, stained teeth and reeking clothes and hair... you are fitter, healthier, more attractive, more energetic. More Alive.

As a non-smoker, you no longer look for self confidence, for self esteem, for ways of coping with problems, in packs of cigarettes. You are now aware that good feelings about yourself and your life come from deep within. Not from sticks of poisonous weed.

You see yourself now as a confident and self-assured nonsmoker... proud of your achievement. Those around you who continue to smoke do not concern you. You wish them the same good feelings and freedom that you now experience... the newfound reality that is Your Life, without the need or desire for the destructive effects of cigarettes. To them you express a gentle and understanding indifference, coupled with your own firm resolve as you express and assert yourself always as that person who has no need or desire for cigarettes.

You can be intensely aware of the pride in your achievement each time you refuse cigarettes, and should you ever, through mistake or childish impulse, ever put a cigarette to your lips ever again... your subconscious mind will remind you in a powerful and unmistakeable way... of the nauseating smell, of the vile disgusting taste and of the guilt that attends each and every cigarette. You will be reminded of your responsibility that cannot be passed on to any other person. Your health. Your life. Your body. Your commitment to yourself and those who love and care for you and who rely on you to be there.

Now today is the right time to free yourself forever from smoking, aware that your subconscious mind knows what to do for you, automatically for you... every morning, waking bright and fresh, with No Need Or Desire To Smoke, travelling to work, or walking the dog, or visiting friends, with No Need Or Desire To Smoke, in the pub, or out to lunch, with No Need Or Desire To Smoke, after a meal, or out for a drink, with No Need Or Desire To Smoke, enjoying all those things that you have done before, and more, as that person who is comfortable with No Need Or Desire To Smoke. That person who now takes full responsibility for life, for health and happiness, and you can congratulate yourself right now on your excellent achievement, experience now the feeling of deep personal satis-

faction as your confidence and your self-esteem grow and expand.... As your health and fitness improve with each and every new day... that problem finally resolved.

And now you feel so good about yourself that you can imagine on a table in front of you a packet of cigarettes, the ones you used to smoke, that you wasted so much time and money on. Now see a strong wind begin to blow, growing stronger as you watch, stronger and stronger until it is a gale force wind, and see that powerful wind scattering the packet of cigarettes as the contents blow around and disintegrate as you watch, and every trace and every memory of the experience of smoking being swept further and further away into infinity, and with it every small desire to pollute your own body.

And when you can see that the cleansing wind has done its work and all traces and memory of that tobacco have gone completely.... The wind drops, and peace, calm and tranquillity return completely now. You see yourself clearly as a natural non-smoker and you can tell yourself the same. "I am a non-smoker".

Good, very good. A very special part of you remembers clearly the vile taste and the noxious odour of tobacco, strong and intense, and should you ever, through accident or childish, irresponsible impulse, ever put a cigarette near your lips again, that part will provide you with an instant and disgusting reminder that you are a non-smoker, responsible and proud.

Now soon it will be time to emerge from this relaxed state, and before this happens we will add a useful skill to your new *pattern of behaviour, because if you should find yourself in any situation where some element of temptation may cause you to think momentarily in the old way when you used to smoke, it will be useful for you to have a new and innocuous habit to instantly draw a line under any thought or knee-jerk reaction to a social situation or a stressful moment. And so at any time if even the tiniest thought of smoking should cross your mind, you will simply take a deep breath, hold it for a second, and then exhale slowly whilst pushing out and away the thought, and you will do this easily and it will make you feel good, proud and strong that you can easily decide to continue with your new healthy behaviour, with all the amazing benefits that delivers for you and those who care about you. And each time you take a deep breath, anytime, anywhere, you can allow small waves of smug satisfaction to stimulate your pleasure centres, because you won, you beat the old habit and gave way to new and beneficial behaviour which can easily last for the rest of your life.*

So now take a few moments of quietness to allow these new learnings to filter throughout your mind and body, and feel how good it feels to have won. Enjoy the sensation of relaxation and triumph, because you so thoroughly deserve a reward for the work you have done here, and just relax.

13

OTHER USES FOR SELF-HYPNOSIS

Weight Loss

The professional hypnotherapy approach to weight loss can take a number of forms, using some or all of the following therapeutic steps;

Patient Classification: "Mindless Dieter", "Mindless Over-Eater", and "Mindless Chaotic Eater" are three typical categories which can be helped by hypnosis. "Mindless Under-Eater" is a more specialised area, not suitable for self-intervention.

Keeping A Food Log: Over-eaters are often mildly self-delusional, in as much as they think that they are eating normal amounts, but may have a blind-spot to a lot of supplementary snacking that takes place (hence the use of "Mindless")

Underlying Causes: Over-eating may often be rooted in psychological causes dating back to early life. Family habits during childhood can have a powerful effect on someone's own behaviour as an adult.

Confidence and Self-Control Issues: Many over-eaters use food as a comfort position, trying to satisfy cravings for unfulfilled emotional requirements. The chocolate industry has built much of its fortune on this! Other people simply crave the 'fullness' feeling that comes with over-eating, and have not been able to develop the disciplines and strategies to resist. Hypnotherapy seeks out and deals with these motivators very effectively.

'Lunch Effect' Many people gravitate towards lunchtime as a haven of relief or reward, because of their job or workplace. Lunchtime is a break in the monotony, or a chance to catch up with friends and colleagues, or even just an excuse to leave the office. The problem is that an entire industry has been built on providing high-carb and high-sugar lunch options.

People tend to over-order and/or over-consume at lunchtime because of an inherent fear of feeling hungry in the afternoon, or some misplaced belief that they need to boost energy levels to get through to five-thirty. Carbs and sugars (such as sandwiches and burger buns) certainly do provide a boost to short-term energy, but inevitably cause a crash after a few hours, which leaves you tired and empty, and craving more food.

Weight loss is a highly personalised intervention when done by a hypnotherapist. Everyone has a different combination of issues, so the combination of treatment techniques can vary widely. However, here are some of the common elements that you can use:

- The food log is something you can do for yourself, which will at the very least show you just how much you're actually eating. There are numerous apps on the iTunes and Android stores to enable you to use your smartphone to manage the tracking, and these can give you relatively accurate calorie counts and nutritional values.
- Like all aspects of dieting, the key element is your commitment. You can have all the gadgets and systems you like, but you must make a *total commitment* to keeping up the discipline, if you're going to succeed. You can use your self-hypnosis techniques to help you with this. I recommend that you find time each morning to drop into trance and give yourself lots of reinforcement and encouragement.
- Keep things simple. Visualise how you want to look, or the life you want to lead, and see yourself in that situation as if it is in the

present tense. If you do this each day, the imagery will become part of who you actually are, not just who you want to be, and you will have a powerful support system to get you through each day. That is the basis of many hypnotherapist weight-loss interventions.

You can also use your self-hypnosis techniques in the following ways:

- When you crave food outside of conventional mealtimes, find a quiet place and drop into trance. Use a one liner such as: *"When it's the right time to eat, I will enjoy my nutritional meal and eat only as much as my body needs"*.
- Before you head out to a restaurant, use a trance to visualise the meal you will order and consume, and the items you'll decline or refuse, such as the bread-basket, the potatoes, chips or fries, and the dessert course. Nobody ever died from eating less sugar and starch!
- Organised weight-loss programmes, such as Weight Watchers, are phenomenally successful. Weight Watchers is a huge global organisation which only profits if its clients succeed, so it has invested millions in developing systems based on the psychology

of weight loss, particularly peer-group encouragement and structured systems.

- If you are, for whatever reason, unable or unwilling to try a group-based approach or consult a professional hypnotherapist, you might consider my audio hypnosis program called *The Determination Diet* which you'll find at ricksmithhypnosis.com.

But in the end, it really just boils down to two things; *cut out the carbs and exercise more*, and you will lose weight. Guaranteed!

Time Compression

Sometimes you find yourself in a situation where you just wish you had a time machine, so that a particular experience or situation could be over! Self-hypnosis is a great way to do it!

A few years ago, I was on vacation in the Gulf of Thailand. I was transferring by speedboat between Koh Tao and Koh Samui in very rough seas, a thoroughly unpleasant journey of around two hours. The boat was overcrowded, the waves were lashing over us, and everyone was being sick over the side. I don't think I've found myself in such a miserable and frightening situation, before or since. Faced with the option of suffering the interminable experience or finding an alternative, I successfully dropped myself into trance for the duration of the trip. I can't remember anything more about the journey, though my travelling companions looked and sounded dreadful when we reached our destination.

I've subsequently adapted this technique for use on short-haul flights, as a method of 'zoning out' from the noise and discomfort, especially a coach-class middle seat, and it works really well.

You can use your self-hypnosis induction in any situation, and an airline seat is perfect because you're forced to sit in one position for a couple of hours. It works best if you can block out the noise; earplugs are the best. You don't particularly need any objectives to work on in trance: I find that once I'm under I can just let my mind wander and explore all sorts of subjects that I simply don't have time to think about during the course of a normal day. You also don't need to worry about emerging yourself, because the plane will usually do that for you when it touches down! Just remember not to recline your seat, so the cabin crew won't disturb you during preparations for landing.

You can also experiment with music. I carry a special playlist in my iPhone for just this purpose. The first track is a long dreamy piece of music which is ideal for self-induction, then there are around twenty of my favourite songs, and once I'm in trance I can use the music to trigger endorphin releases (the 'thrill' chemical). If you practice, you will be able to do this. I learned it by visualising a big red button which I can press any time I like, and when it's pressed, it releases a blast of endorphins, which feels great. The only notes of caution I would place on this technique are these; firstly, you will probably be grinning like a Cheshire Cat throughout the flight, and secondly it can be quite draining if you keep it going for too long.

If you want something simpler, try using the *Beach* script we practiced earlier. It's only about fifteen minutes, but it will give you a good taster for time-compression, and no good trance ever goes unrewarded!

Try Things Out For Yourself

Armed with the skills you've now learned and practiced, and the sample applications in the past few chapters, you should now be in a good position to use self-hypnosis for many different and useful things.

Remember, by placing yourself in trance, you can communicate directly with your subconscious mind, where habits and behaviours are learned, stored and managed. Hypnosis in general, and self-hypnosis in particular, is a powerful way to effect change in yourself.

Here are a few more things you might consider, if they

apply to you. You know how to write one-line suggestions, so don't be afraid to try.

- You're nervous, ahead of an interview or a meeting. Try self-hypnosis to calm yourself and relax, whilst focusing on the key objectives. Visualise the successful outcome and experience how it feels to succeed, then go and do it!
- You want to improve your sporting performance. Use trance to visualise the way you want it to go, and then simply repeat the actions once you start the game.
- You're going on a date, and you're nervous about letting yourself down, maybe by saying the wrong thing. Hypnotise yourself and imagine the perfect evening, how calm and charismatic you will be. Always visualise in the present tense, as if it's actually happening. Use this as a rehearsal, because preparation is always the best way to ensure perfect performance.
- You're learning a script or practicing a presentation. If you find you can't remember a word or phrase, drop quickly into trance and go deep inside. If it's in there, you'll find it. This *memory recall* technique need only take a

few seconds, but the more you practice it, the easier and more successful it will be, and it's a great secret weapon to have in your armoury.

Take every opportunity to practice going in and out of trance, and each time you do you will find that it becomes easier to attain and you can go deeper than the time before.

Most of all, however you use it, enjoy it!

ADDITIONAL RESOURCES

The Scripts Used in this Book

The three main scripts we used in Section One can be streamed or downloaded free once you register at

http://tiny.cc/mshpbreg

If you encounter any issues obtaining the recordings, please e-mail me and I'll fix it for you.

rick@ricksmithhypnosis.com

Contact Details

Of course, I would encourage you to interact with me on any aspect of self-hypnosis, or anything else you come across in this book. There's a Facebook Page called 'ricksmithhypnosis' which allows you to post comments and suggestions, and it's a great place to tell others about your experiences with self-hypnosis.

You can register for updates, ask questions or leave comments, and from time to time you'll find additional scripts available for you to download and use.

If you enjoy the book and you find something worth-while in the system, please take a moment to post a Review, so others can discover the magic of hypnosis.

However you decide to use your new skills, above all: *enjoy the journey!*

Rick Smith

Cape Town, 11th February 2018.

Made in the USA
Monee, IL
11 July 2020